Series "Innovation in den Hochschulen:
Nachhaltige Entwicklung"
Edited by
Gerd Michelsen, Andreas Fischer und Ute Stoltenberg

No. 8:
COPERNICUS in Lüneburg
Higher Education in the Context of
Sustainable Development and Globalization

**Bd. 8 der Reihe „Innovation in den Hochschulen:
Nachhaltige Entwicklung"**
Herausgegeben von
Gerd Michelsen, Andreas Fischer und Ute Stoltenberg

Die Reihe „Innovation in den Hochschulen: Nachhaltige Entwicklung" will die Informationen und Erfahrungen im Rahmen eines universitären Agendaprozesses weitergeben. Konsequenzen einer nachhaltigen Entwicklung für den Innovationsprozess an Hochschulen sollen zur Diskussion gestellt werden. Ziel ist eine ausführliche Auseinandersetzung darüber in Wissenschaft und Öffentlichkeit. Ausgangspunkt für die verschiedenen Veröffentlichungen in der Reihe ist das Projekt „Agenda 21 und Universität Lüneburg". Die Reihe wird herausgegeben von Prof. Dr. Andreas Fischer, Prof. Dr. Gerd Michelsen und Prof. Dr. Ute Stoltenberg, Universität Lüneburg.

**No. 8 of the series "Innovation in den Hochschulen:
Nachhaltige Entwicklung"**
Edited by
Gerd Michelsen, Andreas Fischer und Ute Stoltenberg

The book series "Innovation in den Hochschulen: Nachhaltige Entwicklung" (Innovation in Higher Education: Sustainable Development) provides information and experiences on sustainability in higher education. The several publications highlight the implications of sustainable development for innovation in higher education institutions. The objective is a critical reflection in science and with the public-at-large. The project "Agenda 21 und Universität Lüneburg" constitutes the basis for this book series. The series is edited by Prof. Dr. Andreas Fischer, Prof. Dr. Gerd Michelsen und Prof. Dr. Ute Stoltenberg, all Lüneburg University.

Rietje van Dam-Mieras, Gerd Michelsen,
Hans-Peter Winkelmann (Eds.)

COPERNICUS in Lüneburg

**Higher Education in the Context of
Sustainable Development and Globalization**

Bibliographic information published by Die Deutsche Bibliothek

Die Deutsche Bibliothek lists this publication in the Deutsche National-
bibliografie; detailed bibliographic data is available in the Internet at
http://dnb.ddb.de.

Das Projekt „Agenda 21 und
Universität Lüneburg" wird
gefördert durch die Deutsche
Bundesstiftung Umwelt.

© 2002 VAS – Verlag für Akademische Schriften
Alle Rechte vorbehalten.

Herstellung: VAS, Wielandstraße 10, 60318 Frankfurt am Main
Vertrieb: Koch, Neff & Oettinger & Co. – Verlagsauslieferung
GmbH, Stuttgart
Umschlag: Nach einem Entwurf von Stefan Behrens

Printed in Germany • ISBN 3-88864-357-0

Content

Preface 9

I. Higher Education and Sustainable Development

M. C. E. (Rietje) van Dam-Mieras, Gerd Michelsen,
Hans-Peter Winkelmann
Universities, Society and Sustainability 12

M. C. E. (Rietje) van Dam-Mieras
Sustainable Development: the Interdependence of Different
Domains 19

Leo Jansen
System Innovation for Sustainability in Europe:
the Contribution of Higher Education 33

II. Sustainability and Education

M. C. E. (Rietje) van Dam-Mieras
Reflections on Learning and Sustainable Development 58

John Fien
Teacher Education for Sustainability: A Case Study of the
UNESCO Multimedia Teacher Education Programme 71

Rietje van Dam-Mieras, Ron Corvers,
Hans-Peter Winkelmann
ICT and Working Together at a Distance: European Virtual
Seminar on Enlargement and Sustainable Development 92

Marie-Claude Roland, Anne-Marie Chevre, Joël Chadœuf,
Bernard Hubert, Joseph Bonnemaire
Think Forward, Act Now: Training Young Researchers for
Sustainability. Reshaping the Relationship between PhD
Student and Adviser 98

Wilfried P.M.F. Ivens
New Ways of Academic Education:
Chances for Sustainability 111

III. Translating Theory into Practice

Gerd Michelsen
Higher Education and Sustainable Development in Germany:
The Example of the University of Lüneburg............................... 120

Emanuel Rogier van Mansvelt
The Dutch Example: A Bottom-up Approach to Integrating
Sustainable Development in Higher Education 134

*Heloise Buckland, Fiona Brookes, Deborah Seddon,
Andy Johnston, Sara Parkin*
The UK Higher Education Partnership for
Sustainability (HEPS) 150

Piera Ciceri, Camilla Bargellini, Fausta Setti
A Network of Knowledge and Practices for Sustainability: an
Italian Project Linking University, School System and Local
Community through Participation to Agenda 21 Processes 160

Wynn Calder, Richard M. Clugston
U.S. Progress Toward Sustainability in Higher Education 171

IV. Ways to Institutionalize the Concepts

Peter Blaze Corcoran and Emanuel Rogier van Mansvelt
On the Meaning of Institutional Commitment and
Institutional Assessment 200

Peter Blaze Corcoran
The Earth Charter: An Ethical Framework for "Good"
Globalization 213

Hans-Peter Winkelmann
COPERNICUS-CAMPUS – The University Network for
Sustainability in Europe 220

V. Appendix

The role of universities in agenda 21 239

Declarations on Sustainability in Universities
    A. COPERNICUS University Charter for Sustainable
       Development 240
    B. The Kyoto Declaration 242
    C. The Talloires Declaration 244
    D. The Lüneburg Declaration on Higher Education for
       Sustainable Development 246

The Global Higher Education for Sustainability Partnership
(GHESP) 249

Authors 252

Preface

Sustainable Development is a complex concept. It not only confronts ecological sustainability and economic development, it also tries to reconcile them.

From the ecological perspective it is important to realise that the ecological systems of the earth are the substrate that link both geographically remote places and present and future generations. Because of the rapid developments in the transport of persons, physical goods and information in the last decades our economy has become global. Production systems are increasingly geographically spread and a life cycle assessment of products will make clear that decisions taken from en ecological perspective in one part of the world may have social-economic consequences in other parts of the world.

From the economic perspective it should be remarked that economic growth is considered to be important for human and societal development and welfare, but it has its negative external effects at, for instance, the level of ecosystems which must be dealt with. The latter is an extremely difficult task which asks for innovations in both the fields of technology and social sciences. Human creativity is of vital importance for this.

Sustainable Development thus asks for innovations at a systems level. This implies effects in different types of systems at different levels. It involves the relatively well defined systems that researchers in the field of natural sciences work with, but it also the much more complex systems people in social sciences work with. Systems of the latter type inevitably have to deal with culturally determined norms and values. Sustainable Development also implies action on different levels: the local, the national and the global level. In Sustainable Development al these levels and systems meet. Because of this inherent complexity the process of Sustainable Development will yield different results at different places on earth. Such differences are determined by the specific local conditions. What links all developments, however, is the ecological substrate.

Mankind thus will have to develop a way of living which allows for social and cultural differentiation but at the same time respects the ecological bottom line. In realising these types if innovation at a systems level generation and accessibility ok knowledge and human creativity are of crucial importance. The educational system may be expected to prepare individuals for and support them during this task. Within the educational system higher education has a special place for at least two reasons. It functions on the interface between research and the translation of fundamental knowledge into societal practise on the one hand and it educates the educators of tomorrow on the other. Awareness of these responsibilities are of great importance for the system of higher education. The only available methodology for the innovation process within the higher education system is learning by and while doing. This is the central theme of the book.

The first section of the book deals with the complex concept Sustainable Development. The second section focuses on sustainability and (higher) education. While the third system gives examples of different ways theory can be translated into action in practise, in the last section different ways of institutionalisation of the concept are described.

Finally, we would like to acknowledge with thanks the help of Marco Rieckmann in the editing process of this book.

Heerlen	Rietje van Dam-Mieras
Lüneburg	Gerd Michelsen
Dortmund	Hans-Peter Winkelmann
August 2002	

I.
Higher Education and Sustainable Development

M. C. E. (Rietje) van Dam-Mieras, Gerd Michelsen,
Hans-Peter Winkelmann

Universities, Society and Sustainability

Since the Middle Ages universities have contributed a lot to economic growth and the social welfare of nations. A major asset for their role in society has been the link between research and education. This link was vital for disclosing new knowledge for application in society. Originally main disciplines were theology, law, medicine and philosophy. The latter formed the cradle for the natural sciences, which in their turn provided the basis for technical development.

We could say that in the 17th century a scientific revolution took place which was very important or the development of science and technology and through them for society (Marres and de Vries 2002). From the 17th century on scientific experiments formed a new fundament for knowledge. Ideas, hypotheses and theories were systematically confronted with empirical facts, new instruments were developed and knowledge was spread to society through new scientific journals. This scientific revolution, in its turn, provided a basis for technology development and in this way tightened the link between science and society. Technology development is a result of a process of co-evolution between technical innovations and the social context in which they take place. Mostly technological changes are first embedded in social structures after which the social institutions themselves become liable to change. From that perspective it can be understood that, in addition to technology development, also the practise of protecting intellectual property rights was instrumental for the translation of new knowledge into economically relevant innovations. The development of science and technology lead to a new revolution, known as the Industrial Revolution, which started in the 18th century. This revolution had great social impact in some parts of the world and much less in others.

Especially in those parts of the world presently known as the industrialised countries the influence of natural sciences and technology on economic growth, welfare of nations and individuals, and on societal organisation and institutions has been tremendous. Most citizens in the industrialised parts of the world have a lifestyle based on a knowledge- and energy intensive economy using large amounts of natural resources. The political systems in those parts of the world are more or less democratic and some minimal level of social security is guaranteed by the public domain. Industrialised countries also have rather well developed education systems as knowledge and skills are important items for their labour force.

The educational system is supposed to prepare individuals for their function in society and on the labour market. Target groups for education are children and young adults. A 'classical' learning route could be described as follows (van Dam-Mieras 2002). During their early years children learn a language which enables them to communicate and interact with their environment. During primary and secondary education they learn to understand the complex and changing culture and society, they develop skills which enable them to function in society and they develop independent thinking. After that period further individual development occurs through vocational education, higher education or via other practise embedded opportunities for further development. After this trajectory which takes place, more or less, in institutionalised education, the (young) adults will continue their learning process in practise. The present institutionalised education thus supports learners during certain (early) stages of their learning route.

In the past the social systems in which individuals grew up and functioned were rather stable. They only changed under the influence of compelling external factors. However, nowadays because of, among others, the influence of globalisation and the developments in information and communication technology (ICT), continuous change seems to be the most constant factor. The originally rather stable system has changed in an arrangement in which changes are continuously and intrinsically present. Individuals must find their own way in interaction with that complex social environment. Therefore the educational system should learn people to think independently and enable them to choose their own way. The educational system can no longer be uniform, the ideal learning environment must be dynamic and must do justice, as much as possible, to the affinity and talents of each individual. The educational system therefore will have to learn how to cope with a large heterogeneity of talents, social, economical and cultural backgrounds.

Another consequence of the fact that changes in our global society are continuous is that the learning of individuals must continue after leaving the educational system. In the past that learning took place in practise, but nowadays the rapid changes in society ask for (a certain degree of) institutionalisation of the life long learning process. Universities and institutions of higher and vocational education are obvious candidates to play a role in that respect.

The developments described above took place largely on a national basis. However, because of highly improved international transport facilities for persons, goods, information and services, our daily life no longer takes place only at a national level. Although we physically live, most of the time, at specific places were we have roots in families, regions and cultures, the economic system is global and for European citizens laws and regulations are more and more developed at the European level. Therefore we feel that the growth towards democracy that took place at a national scale in the preceding centuries will have to be repeated at a global scale. Different actors will be involved and the process of development will have different formats at different locations in the world. Governments, companies, non governmental organisations (NGO's) and citizens will have to find out how life in this global environment can be organised in such a way that it enables communities in one part of the world to choose the life style they want respecting at the same time the autonomy of other communities to do so as well. The global community certainly will be heterogeneous, but we can and may not deny that it is emerging, whatever its appearance will be. One very important, perhaps even the most important, question in this respect is how do we reconcile ecological sustainability and economic growth? Put in other words: How do we organise sustainable development?

Sustainable development is a complex concept in which a broad range of stakeholders are involved (see also the contribution of Leo Jansen in this book). Sustainable development asks for changes at a systems level. It implies both the rather well defined physical systems researchers in the natural sciences work with, and the much more complex systems people working in the field of social sciences work with. The latter type of systems inevitably has to deal with culturally determined norms and values. Also different levels are at stake: the local, the national and the global level. Negative external effects at one level can be 'pushed off' to another level. In sustainable development all those different systems and levels meet. In translating the complex concept into practise the ecological, economic, and socio-cultural aspects of different strategies will have to be taken into account. The socio-cultural aspect are about the development op people and their social organisation, the economic aspect relates to economic infrastructure and the efficient management of natural and social resources, and the ecologic aspect focuses on natural ecosystems and natural resources. These different aspects are not easily reconciled, but they can and must not be separated either. Following the fate of a product from the physical resources and energy via the different steps in the production process through the use of the end product to its discharge and recycling, a methodology called Life Cycle Analysis (LCA), will show that in a global economy with geographically spread production processes decisions taken from the ecological perspective in one part of the world may have social economic consequences in other parts of the world. As in the present world that global dimension of our daily life is a fact, intercultural competence is a skill all citizens need. Universities should see it as a task to develop learning environments and methodology that enable individuals to develop such intercultural competences in order to overcome cultural differences.

The concept sustainable development emerged a few decades ago, was formulated in the Brundtland report in 1987 (World Commission on Environment and Development 1987) and was clearly put on the political agenda in Rio the Janeiro in 1992 (anonymus 1992). During the World Summit in Johannesburg in September 2002 it has been discussed in how far we have been successful in realising a more sustainable development since the ambitious Agenda 21 was accepted in Rio the Janeiro. In the past 10 years a lot of activities have been going on, but as was concluded in South Africa it has not been a very great success so far. Perhaps a conclusion could be that we need a new revolution and perhaps another conclusion could be that institutions able to translate new fundamental knowledge into forms of knowledge suitable for solving a broad range of societal problems could be amongst the important actors to bring about the necessary changes. Those institutions could be universities, but in order to meet the challenges successfully these institutions have to reflect on how they can organise their core activities in an innovative way that matches the complex and rapidly changing society of today.

Realising a more sustainable trajectory for the world communities is a tremendous task in which many different actors will have to be involved. Universities could certainly function as a source of inspiration for such a transition because the scientific world is inherently international and ICT offers a lot of tools that could bring a strong international dimension in the learning environment. What we need is a new networked relationship between science and education optimally interacting with a knowledge intensive networked society. Of course universities have to learn how to realise this, in other words, the organisations that offer learning opportunities to individuals should become learning organisations themselves. From this perspective CO-PERNICUS-campus (http://www.copernicus-campus.org) could be considered as a laboratory in which new models for academic co-operation in establishing links between science and education can be developed and evaluated.

From the perspective of sustainable development, it is important to realise that our natural ecosystems are the substrate that links on the one hand our generation to future generations and on the other hand the different parts of the world. This implies that sustainable development trajectories will have different forms determined by the specific contexts. In addition to natural sciences, technology and economy also social and cultural sciences will have to play a role and therefore dealing with sustainable development means dealing with social and cultural differences. One could feel that the European Union, although still struggling with its own enlargement process, is or could be one of the leading domains in the global society. Because of our enlargement process we gather much experience in living together with people from different cultural backgrounds, political systems, ideologies etc. The recent years have shown us how difficult this process of growth is. Of course from the point of view from the member states the perspective on Europe can be twofold. Europe can be seen as a proactive domain in the world and Europe can be seen as a superimposed structure that limits the autonomy and independence of its member states. Taking a global view the perspective of Europe as an active and conscious part of the world and not as a burden on, or restraint to its member states, is more attractive.

Living and working in an academic environment makes it perhaps easier to think in terms of an international community as the international dimension in the scientific world is rather strong. On the other hand, there may be a rather large gap between academic theory and societal practice and perhaps the P3 (People, Profit, Planet) concept underpinning the OECD guidelines for multinational enterprises is more pragmatic (OECD 2000). However, what would be the effect of such guidelines when there was no action in civil society by NGO's operating in the field between science and citizens? The purpose of asking such questions is only to make clear that all those different partners will have to work together in a respectful, transparent and constructive way.

Choosing the perspective of Europe as a developing heterogeneous domain in a networked world community, it would be important for universities to share knowledge and expertise and to adopt a process of cooperative learning how to establish a networked higher education system in a networked Europe to the benefit of all. The direct link between science and education would remain a very important asset for universities, but a flexible network of co-operating universities could be an appropriate answer to the rapidly changing needs of in our complex society. And of course, in a global world, there is no reason to confine the process of building academic partnership to the European Union.

References

Anonymus (1992): Agenda 21, Vols. I, II, III of the report of the United Nations Conference on Environment and Development (Rio de Janeiro, June 1992), Document A/CONF. 151/26, preliminary version of August 1992, United Nations Geneva, 5 Volumes.
Dam-Mieras, M.C.E. (2002): Leren voor het leven, in: van Dam-Mieras, M.C.E./de Jong, W.M. (red.), Onderwijs voor een kennissamenleving. De rol van ICT nader bekeken, Sdu Uitgevers, Den Haag.
Marres, N./de Vries, G. (2002): Tussen toegang en kwaliteit. Legitimatie en contestatie van expertise op het internet in: Dijstelbloem, H./Schuyt, C.J.M. (red.), De publieke dimensie van kennis, Sdu Uitgevers, Den Haag.
OECD (2000): OECD Guidelines for Multinational Enterprises.
World Commission on Environment and Development (1987): Our Common Future, Oxford University Press.

M. C. E. (Rietje) van Dam-Mieras

Sustainable Development: the Interdependence of Different Domains

Introduction

The concept sustainable development was described by the Norwegian prime minister Brundtland in the report *Our Common Future* (1987) as follows: '*Sustainable development is a process of change in which the exploitation of resources, the direction of investments, the orientation of technological development, and the institutional change are all in harmony and enhance both current and future potential to meet human needs and aspirations – (it is) meeting the needs of the present without compromising the ability of future generations to meet their own needs*'. The concept was put on the political agenda by the United Nations Earth Summit held in Rio de Janeiro in 1992. Output of the summit was Agenda 21, the global action plan for sustainable development.

The concept sustainable development emerged from the bringing together of two other concepts: ecological sustainability and economic growth. Ecological sustainability and economic development do not go together easily and technology development functions as the coupling factor. Technology development must be seen as the development of an socio-technical complex. On the one hand technological development makes possible the design of cleaner production systems which decreases the environmental burden, but on the other hand the influence of technology development on social behaviour increases again the environmental burden, in spite of the cleaner technology.

Of course the triangle ecology-economy-technology is embedded in a much broader and very complex context which includes the growth of the world population, the globalisation of the economy, poverty, human security, social equity, democracy, human rights, and peace. However, the positive and negative experience gathered with this triangle during the development of the industrialized world obliges that part of the world to use it as an easy accessible source of inspiration for assisting other countries to reach a more equal share in global prosperity.

Sustainable Development: the Natural Sciences Perspective

In satisfying its needs Mankind uses the earth physical and biological resources and converts them using energy, mostly fossil energy, into a broad range of products. This range of products includes both products necessary to stay alive (the needs) but also products that make life more comfortable (the wants).

Human activities mainly involve the upper layer of the earth, the hydrosphere, and the lower layer of the atmosphere. From these three layers raw materials and energy are withdrawn while waste streams and discharged products are brought into them. From the crust of the earth we obtain for instance coals, oil, gas, metal ores, sulphur, phosphate, sand, gravel, marl, marble, granite and salts. From the hydrosphere we obtain water from springs, sources and precipitation, seawater and salts dissolved therein, and gas hydrates bound to polar ice. From the biosphere we obtain raw materials from plant and animal origin. Almost all energy is either directly or indirectly supplied by the sun. In satisfying its needs Mankind from old has used both its knowledge of the natural system and technology developed using human creativity.

Living organisms, excluding man, withdraw raw materials from their direct environment: carbon dioxide and oxygen from the air, water and elements from soil, larger organic molecules from food, and energy directly (photosynthetic organisms) or indirectly (all other organisms) from the sun. From the energy perspective the net result of living is the conversion of solar energy to biomass. When a living organism dies the active conversion of energy for the production of biomass stops, but the biomass and the energy stored in it are not wasted. During biodegradation other organisms use biomass and stored energy, which results in closed nutrient cycles in living nature. However, biodegradation is not always complete and unders specific geological conditions organic material can be converted into fossil energy (coal, oil, gas), a process that takes million years.

The nutrient cycles described in the preceding paragraph take place at a pace compatible with life. Within system earth these nutrient cycles based on bioconversion are integrated with geochemical cycles which take place on a much longer timescale. The latter encompass the geological processes such as the formation of mountains, erosion, formation of sediments etc.; the energy comes largely from the nuclear reactions taking place within the earth nucleus. As the earth is a closed system the amount of matter is constant and is continuously recycled.

In the large production systems designed by Mankind (agriculture and industry), the focuss normally is on an as high as possible yield of a specific product, and therefore production cycles mostly will not be closed. Because man-designed production processes take place within the closed system earth this implies that the bio-geochemical cycles will be disturbed.

From the foregoing it can be concluded that from the natural sciences perspective key activities for the design of more sustainable production systems are:
- The use of renewable energy
- The closing of bio-geochemical cycles
- The reduction of the amount of raw material used
- The reduction of the amount of material per application

As far as energy is concerned this means investing in renewable energy, preferably by using solar energy directly. For the closing of bio-geochemical cycles this implies that in process design we should not focus on increasing the yield of a specific project, but on closing the cycle from raw material via product and recycling of discharged products as effectively as possible. Biotechnology offers valuable possibilities for innovation in this respect. In addition it can be tried, in analogy with natural ecosystems, to link different production chains so that output of one process can be used as input in another. This approach is known as industrial ecology (Erkman 1997). To reach a reduction in the amount of materials used the further development of molecular sciences and of methods that enable to manipulate, design and produce at a molecular scale is relevant (combinatorial chemistry, nano(bio)technology, bio-informatics). In addition new analytical and separation technology based on molecular knowledge are promising for the improvement of process steering, quality control and monitoring the effect on the environment of production and consumption chains.

Sustainable Development: the Economic Perspective

From the preceding paragraph it can be concluded that natural scientists tend to approach questions of sustainability and scarcity starting from the boundary conditions of system earth. A technological answer to the problems identified can be an increase in the efficiency of the processes of production and consumption (Weaver 2000).

From the economic perspective it is mostly argued that scarcity of resources is a relative, continuously changing concept. It is determined by the technology available for exploitation, transformation and use. The development of new technology can reduce the demand for energy and raw materials, which in turn can stimulate economic growth. However, economic growth should not go hand in hand with effects that increase the environmental burden, which is not a realistic option (Barbiroli 1996). In the economic approach emphasis is on realising possibilities using technological innovations. In addition to technology development also the growth of the world population, the preferences of consumers and prosperity play a role. Very often the negative external effects are not internalised.

The importance of technological development for economic growth is widely recognised, but it should be remarked that until now the economic system developed in a very independent way, seemingly independent of the complex regulation of natural ecosystems. On the one hand economic development has enabled the industrialised part of the world to develop the present lifestyles. On the other hand a price for this development is paid in the growing tension between the human patterns of production and consumption and System Earth. This tension is increasingly manifest at many levels in the global ecosystem. Also the large differences in prosperity and use of the earth's resources between industrialised countries and developing countries are part of it.

The great collaborative challenge remains to realise a development that does justice to both the boundary conditions of System Earth (the natural sciences perspective) and economic development (the economic perspective). A completely sustainable society is not possible on theoretical grounds, but a society that is more sustainable than the present can be realised.

Sustainable Development: the Technological Perspective

Technology development forms an important link between ecological sustainability and economic growth. Production processes can be made more sustainable via technological innovations which reduce the amount of raw materials and fossil energy needed. However, the efforts invested in the innovations trajectory, mostly will not appear for the full 100 % in calculations of the cost price. On the contrary, a cleaner production process in which less raw materials and fossil energy are consumed and less waste is produced, will cause less environmental costs which will reduce the total cost price. As a consequence, the product will be cheaper, the market share will increase and consumption will grow. As a result, in the present institutional setting, the pressure on the environment can grow thanks to cleaner technology. Therefore, a very crucial question is how to make the triangle ecology-economy-technology more sustainable.

Sustainable development asks for strategic technological innovations at the system level. Such innovations are characterised by long development times and much uncertainty. The societal challenge is to develop knowledge, expertise and competencies which enable Mankind to make this change. In this complex of activities technology development will certainly play a role, but the mutual interdependence of technology, culture and institutionalised structures can very effectively block progress towards more sustainability in many arenas (Weaver et al. 2000).

Sustainable Development in Practice: Complex and Difficult

From the foregoing it can be concluded that the concept sustainable development is approached differently from distinct domains. The perspectives reflect the different paradigms in those domains. From the perspective of natural sciences it is mostly argued that the limits to sustainability can be set with more certainty than economists wish to recognise (Ayres 1998). According to Ayres the earth is a complex, interactive, self-organising system, capable of maintaining a stable ordered state far from its thermodynamic equilibrium. The system is able to do so by using solar energy. That energy is captured by photosynthetic organisms and passes within the natural system via biogeochemical cycles. Those cycles are fundamental to the conversion of materials, the flow of materials through the system and nutrient cycles. The latter are of vital importance because life is completely dependent on the nutrient cycles within System Earth.

The biosphere thus forms a vital active regulatory element within the system. Because the system is not linear the dynamic behaviour is potentially chaotic. The ordered state of the system depends on the occurrence of feedback loops between its processes. In order for those feedback loops to function the system should remain between certain limits. Therefore the stability of the system can be threatened by major changes in the climate, a loss of biodiversity, deforestation, desertification, accumulation of toxic heavy metals and of non-degradable compounds in soils and sediments. The main trends that cause such disturbances are: the continuing growth of the world population, the increasing demand for raw materials used in industrial activity, the emission of waste and pollution from economic activity and anthropogenic disturbance of natural ecosystems.

Ayres discriminates between non-controversial items such as the growth of the world population and the concern for resources, and controversial items such as pollution, productivity and the stability of the biosphere. Ayres translates his considerations in three targets for the 21st century. In the first place the use of fossil fuels should be reduced to very low levels. In the second place a reflection on and adaptation of large scale production systems such as agriculture, forestry and fishery is needed. In the third place the net emission to the environment of heavy metals and non-degradable compounds should be reduced to almost zero.

However, in practice limits to societal activity are not set from the natural sciences perspective. Instead, limits are set by the complex dynamic interaction in which, in addition to the environmental capacity, technological capacity, institutional capacity, ideology and culture all play a role. Most people are not only aimed at fulfilling their basic needs, they also want, if they can afford, products that make life more pleasant. This latter category is determined by personal preferences and by what is technologically feasible and economically affordable. There will be a co-evolution of their demands with technological development and prosperity.

Sustainable Development: Consumers Behaviour

The dynamics of consumption processes are determined by the supply of products on the market and the possibility of consumers to buy those products. Both are in the end determined by the interplay between activities in the production and service sector and law and regulations produced by national and local governments. In the first domain the globalisation of the economy is an important factor, in the second the international cooperation between countries within supranational structures.

The characteristics of the market economy generate continuous technological development. Competition between companies leads on the one hand to a reduction of cost price and on the other to product diversification. In both technology based innovations play a role.
The majority of product innovations concerns an adaptation of already existing products. The development criteria for each product are partly determined by the specific character of the product and partly by more general aspects such as consumers comfort, efficiency and control. Also the environmental friendliness can be part of the design criteria. However, most changes are not inspired by environmental concern but rather driven by the target of increasing turnover.

In the situation described above technological innovation leads to the continuous improvement existing products. Sometimes the innovation has more drastic consequences, however. New fundamental knowledge can lead to key technologies that can be applied in many different products and processes. This will lead to a large amount of innovations in different sectors of the economy, which will in the end influence the daily life op households. ICT constitutes an example of such a key technology, modern biotechnology probably is another one.

Radical innovations mostly 'emerge' as specialised applications in specific niches in the market. Those new products are, mostly for financial reasons, only obtained by a small amount of consumers. By using it these consumers are testing the product and thereby contribute to financing its improvement and reducing production costs. In a next stage the adapted product can be sold on a larger market.

Consumer goods contribute to the social identity of the consumer (Røpke 2001). As the social identity is determined by the interaction of the individual with the physical and social environment, consumer goods are part of a cultural information system. According to Røpke in the interaction between technology driven innovations and the continuous confirmation of social identity two dilemma's play a role, at least in industrialised countries. The first dilemma is that of the family: the tension between the coherence between family members on the one hand and the realisation of the goals of individual family members on the other. The second is the dilemma of the domains: in the present industrialised society social life is differentiated and each individual participates in different domains, which results in conflicts between domains (work, family life, recreation). Using technology based consumer goods the individual tries to fit all activities into daily life thereby increasing the intensity of experiences per unit of time.

Of course technological designers have ideas about possible applications of a product and about its cultural meaning, but a product will be developed further during its use in practice. That product development in daily life is influenced by social structures and cultural conceptions in households. This process of interaction between technology and households will not only result in adaptation of product design, it will also result in an adaptation of daily life in households. Technology and households thus change in continuous mutual interaction. The other side of the same coin is that companies will focus on continuous adaptation to consumer demands and on shorter product life cycles (Sonntag 2000). In general, the interaction between technology and consumption dynamics will contribute to consumption growth and thus to an increase in the pressure on the natural environment.

Sustainble Development: People, Profit, Planet

Both the public sector and the private sector perceive sustainable development as an important long term issue. It is part of the *Guidelines for Multinational Enterprises* accepted by the OECD member states in 2000 (OECD 2000). The governments encourage multinational enterprises to live up to the Guidelines in all countries were they are active while respecting specific conditions in each host country. The recommendations are based on principles and norms of good behaviour in accordance with law and regulations. Living up to the Guideline by companies occurs on a voluntary basis. Governments of OECD member states that signed the Guidelines are obliged to promote their use. They will create national contact points which promote the use of the Guidelines, function as a discussion forum and participate in evaluation- and advice procedures.

The formulation of the *Guidelines for Multinational Enterprises* by the OECD member states is of course inspired by the globalisation of the economy. With the rise of service and knowledge intensive economy large scale international mergers became a trend and companies operating at a multinational scale became involved in different types of joint ventures and organisational structures. Strategic alliances and closer relations with suppliers and subcontractors render the boundaries of the company more diffuse. Those structural changes in multinational companies also influence their activities in developing countries. In the past their focus in those countries was mainly on primary production and raw materials, but presently they are involved with diversified activities like manufacturing, assembling, market development and services.

The globalisation of the economy not only influences multinational companies, also the foreign investments of small and medium sized companies are becoming more important and also for these companies the boundaries between company and environment become less sharp. Therefore the OESO Guidelines in fact apply to good behaviour of all enterprises.

An enterprise can be described as a profit oriented organisation whose relations with the external environment are organised via markets (SER 2000). De boundaries between the enterprise and its environments can be visualised as the result of a trade off between pro's and con's of co-ordination via organisation within the enterprise and co-ordination by the market. Organising activities within the enterprise results in savings on the transaction costs and in a bundling of production factors within the organisation for a longer period. An enterprise thus can be described as an organisation for long term co-operation of the different stakeholders involved.

Enterprises create value by producing and selling goods and services which contribute to satisfying needs and to societal prosperity. Their activities also generate income for entrepreneurs, employees and shareholders. However, they not only create values, by their activities they can also damage ore destroy values such as environmental values and welfare. Of course the net effect of entrepreneurial activities should not be reduced to financial profits for owners, employees and shareholders. Entrepreneurial activities should be seen as social activities and therefore the enterprise can be held responsible for the effects of its activities to society. Responsible entrepreneurship therefore may not be reduced to complying with law and regulations and charity, responsible behaviour towards society should constitute an essential part of entrepreneurship. Long term societal prosperity and a transparent and respectful relationship with the different shareholders involved are core values in that respect.

Responsible entrepreneurship implies a deliberate targeting of the activities on long term value creation in three dimensions:
- People: the result of the activities for employees and people in the company environment
- Profit: bringing forth goods and services with profit as a sign of social appreciation of the activities
- Planet: the effect of the activities on the natural environment

Conclusion: Sustainable Development Learning while Doing?

A more sustainable development depends on set of interdependent changes in economic structure, profiles of productions and consumption, technology and institutions. Research has shown that eco-restructuring has far-reaching consequences for the demand for labour and capital, for production geography, for patterns of consumption, for the environmental burden, and for the division of economical and political power (Simonis 1994). Eco-restructuring implies a change in paradigm. A development trajectory in which environmental capital and environmental profits are factors of relatively minor importance should be transformed into a development trajectory in which safeguarding of environmental capital is a fundamental design criterion.

This conclusion may sound rather logic, but real life is so obstinate. Some people will be concerned about having enough food for their family and about the absence of very basic medical care. Others may be concerned about modern biotechnology in relation to food safety or ethical issues around gene therapy. Many people will be concerned about violent conflicts, human security, poverty, human rights and democracy. Because of the complexity and global dimension of the problem most people might feel rather powerless.

Yet the problem is not new. In 1798 the English vicar and economist Malthus stated in his *Essay on the principles of population and its effects on human happiness* that war, starvation and disasters would continuously reduce the world population to a level in agreement with the available means. Not all people shared his views in those days. The French mathematician, pedagogue and politician Condorcet (*Esquisse d'un tableau historique des progress de l'esprit humain*, 1794) and the English writer and theoretical politician Godwin (*Enquiry concerning political justice and its influence on general virtue and happiness*, 1793) had the opinion that the progress of knowledge and technology would bring Mankind prosperity and chances for personal development. In retrospection we could say that they all were right to some extent; the perception certainly will be influenced by that part of the world you are thinking of.

An important question we are left with after such considerations is: 'Are we able to learn from the past, both at the individual and the collective level, in order to contribute to a more sustainable future?' Of course a more sustainable future is a long term value for all of us, but would you be so concerned about it if all your energy was needed to survive the present?

References

Ayres, R. (1998): Ecorestructuring : the transition to an ecologically sustainable economy, in: Ayres, R./Weaver, P. (eds.), Ecorestructuring: implications for sustainable development, Tokyo, United Nations University Press.

Barbiroli, G. (1996): The role of technology and science in sustainable development, in: Nath, B./Hens, L./Devuyst, D. (eds.), Sustainable development, VUBPRESS Brussel, pp 313-349.

Erkman, S. (1997): Industrial ecology: an historical view, J. Cleaner Prod. 5, 1-1?.

OECD (2000): OECD Guidelines for Multinational Enterprises.

Røpke, I. (2001): New technology in everyday life - social processes and environmental impact, Ecological Economics, 38, 403-422.

SER (2000): De winst van waarden, The Hague.

Simonis, U. (1994): Industrial restructuring in industrial countries, in: Ayres, R./Weaver, P. (eds.), Ecorestructuring: implications for sustainable development, Tokyo, United Nations University Press.

Sonntag, V. (2000): Sustainability – in light of competitiveness, Ecological Economics 34, 101-113.

Weaver, P./Jansen, L./van Grootveld, G./van Spiegel, E./Vergragt, Ph. (2000): Sustainable technology development, Greenleaf publishing, Sheffield, UK.

World Commission on Environment and Development (1987): Our Common Future, Oxford University Press.

Leo Jansen

System Innovation for Sustainability in Europe: the Contribution of Higher Education[1]

Introduction

Since the WECD reported on Sustainable Development in "Our common future" (World Commission on Environment and Development 1987) as a basis for the World Conference on the Environment in Rio de Janeiro (1992) with the Agenda 21 as a result, many visions, reports, plans on different levels up to the EU, OECD and UNO and from different sources: Governments, Science, Industrial Organisations, NGO's have from different points of view given views on strategies and measures supporting the process of sustainable development. In many sectors of the economy, impressive results on conservation of the environment and on prevention of future damage have been achieved. Three trajectories of change can be distinguished (but not separated): "optimisation – improvement - renewal". In each of these trajectories a specific interaction between "culture, structure and technology" can be recognised. In the process of sustainable development "Optimisation" and "Improvement" with respect to environment have been practised and developed in the last decades supported in policy programs and industrial initiatives gathering the "low hanging fruits". Nevertheless hardly any options for breakthroughs to the necessary renewal of development to a sustainable development were opened. The complexity of the social and political processes necessary to initiate breakthroughs may be a severe thresholds. To open such future

---

1   This chapter refers to a presentation held at the COPERNICUS-Conference "The Role of Higher Education for Sustainability: Towards the World Summit for Sustainable Development", University of Lüneburg, 8–10 October 2001.

options innovation processes have to be initiated on the basis of a clear understanding of the challenges and acceptance of crucial values behind the process.

In the end three questions have to be answered:
- What: Which actions and policies of transition in private and public have to be undertaken to achieve a sustainable future for Europolis by and fundamental (technology) system renewal?
- How: Which process, by whom, could break through the inertia in an evolutionary way to initiate a broad supported movement to achieve these actions and policies?
- When: When will the combination of urgency of development and the time necessary for (fundamental) change induce the urgency of action?

On a national scale experiences have been gained in general integrated foresight programs for economic development with time scales up to about 15 years. These programs learn how to organise co-operation between private parties, public parties and science. The degree of taking sustainable development into account differs from the one to the other. However a Dutch experience learns that to achieve renewal the time scale has to be stretched up to decades and that backcasting approaches (from need to product, and from future to present) are means to develop creative jump like approaches which at the same time open profitable short term opportunities. A 7-step iterative and interactive approach proved to be practicable for different sectors in the Netherlands.

The rules for the architecture of innovation processes for renewal ranging from small scale up to supranational may be designed by combining experiences gained up to now. Integration of different domains of knowledge (disciplines, sectors, institutions) proves to be essential to obtain viable results and broadly supported development processes. The architecture should bridge a number of sincere dilemmas and describe the necessary attitudes of actors and stakeholders to initiate substantial innovation processes.

The next question is whether and how the policies can be directed to initiate innovation processes to develop sustainable options for the future. On the basis of a general future orientation on the EU level a framework for innovation processes in respectively domains of need, in economic sectors and in different regions can be developed. Policies to initiate such innovation processes should recognise a double approach: top-down and bottom–up. Changes in societal systems and changes in governmental structures and procedures may run parallel in the sequence "optimisation – improvement - renewal". Depending on time scales roles of Industry, Science and Technology, NGO's and Government can be described.

A proposal for a step-wise process to break through the inertia in an evolutionary way is given.

The Challenge of Sustainable Development

"Fulfilling peoples needs of the present and future generations" according to the Brundtland report (World Commission on Environment and Development 1987) requires actions on short, medium and long term. "Future generations" may be supposed to be three generations, the scope people usually cover with their experience and affinity to future generations. Three generations cover a period of about 50 years. Considering the almost unavoidable growth of the world population, the desired growth of welfare per capita in North and South (RIO 21) and the desired (or "necessary") reduction of environmental pressure from local up to global scales, sustainable development to fulfil peoples needs requires radical improvement of the eco-efficiency (depending on assumptions and on specific need ranging from a factor five up to fifty). Such requirement demands for fundamental renewal of (technology) systems to provide these needs. As fundamental system renewal takes several decades of time from "concept to market", initiation of renewing innovation on the shortest possible time is utmost urgent.

SUSTAINABLE DEVELOPMENT: THE GLOBAL CHALLENGE		
Population	↑	2
Prosperity	↑	5
Pressure on Ecosystem	↓	2
Ecoefficiency	↑	20

Figure 1: The challenge of sustainable development

Dimensions of Change

In the process of change to achieve a sustainable Development three interacting dimensions can be distinguished:

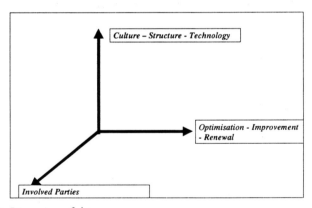

Figure 2: Dimensions of change

Interwovenness of "Culture – Structure - Technology"

The eco-efficiency-improvements should be achieved for the whole of means fulfilling peoples needs varying from simple items up to complex technological systems. This achievement requires intensive

interacting changes in culture, (institutional) structure and technology:
- culture, legitimating nature conditions and volume of societal needs to be fulfilled: sufficiency,
- structure, the economic and institutional organisation to fulfil legitimated needs: effectivety,
- technology, providing the technical means by which needs are (to be) fulfilled: efficiency.

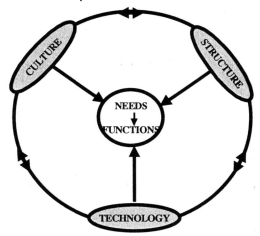

Figure 3: Interwovenness of Culture, Structure and Technology

Trajectories: Optimisation
– Improvement and Redesign – Renewal

Improvement of eco-efficiency has to be fitted within the time scope business and governance is accustomed to for usual decisions and actions, as well as within the current situation. This reflects in a threefold approach along parallel trajectories (figure 4):
- System Optimisation, corresponding to operational processes like quality management, maintenance, auditing, efficiency drives etc, all with time scales up to 5 years maximum and with an expected effect on eco-efficiency ranging up to a factor 1.5.

- System Improvement, leaving fundamental structures and technologies unchanged but implementing incremental changes corresponding to processes like revision, reorganisation, redesign with time scales from 5 to 20 years and with an expected effect on eco-efficiency ranging from a factor 1.5 up to 5.
- System Renewal, by fundamental jump-like changes, resulting from long term research and affecting structure, culture and technology fundamentally, with time scales of over 20 years. Drastic renewal of technology means: redefining actual technology development trajectories and provoking new ones aiming at increases of the eco-efficiency by a factor 5 to 50, with a "factor 20" as a target (to begin with for developed countries).

The time scales of these trajectories correspond to the time scope of actions as well as to the time scope of their results.

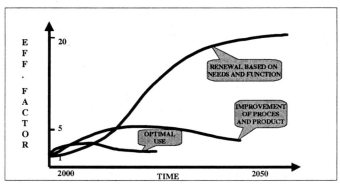

Figure 4: Trajectories of change in sustainable development

Parties Involved

The ambition of System Renewal can only be realised in co-operation between relevant stake holders which can be grouped in:
- Governmental bodies,
- Private producing parties,

- Science & Technology,
- NGO's including consumers.

These parties act in their own arena and are accounted for in their own currency (Vasbinder/Groen). To ensure their participation in the process of Systems Renewal they should be able to recognise the possibility to gain profits in their arena. At the same time the parties should have trust in the balance of positions.

Table 1: Arena and currencies for parties in sustainable development

	Parties			
	Private production	Science & Technology	NGO's	Government
Arena	Market	Scientific world	Public	Politics
Currency	Bottom-line Earnings	Recognition	Influence and support	Power

In the process of System Renewal the specific responsibilities, attitudes and term of action have to be taken into account.

Table 2: Characteristics of parties in sustainable development

	Relevant aspects with respect to SD		
	Responsibility	Attitude	Terms of Action
Market/ Private Parties	Exploration of opportunities	Active Short	
Science & Techn.	Analysis, Description	Active	Short
	Design	Active	Long
NGO's	Norm Setting	Active	Short
	Vision Development	Active	Long
Governments	Control	Reactive to private parties	Short
	Planning	Reactive to NGO's and Science	Long

The interactions of these dimensions of change result into different characatisations of actions and involved actors as shown in figure.

Table 3: Culture-Structure-Technology in subsequent trajectories of development

	OPTIMISATION	IMPROVEMENT	RENEWAL
CULTURE	CAREFULNESS THRIFTINESS Disciplined	AMBITIOUS PRO-ACTIVE INITIATIVE TAKING	VISIONAIRY SWEEPING INTEGRAL
STRUCTURE	COST SAVING REGULATIVE IMAGE BUILDUNG	SECTORAL COOPERATIVE CHAIN PRINCIPLE PROGRESSIVE REGULATION	"INTER-INTER" COOPERATIVE NICHE-POLICIES
TECHNOLOGY	RECYCLING ENERGY EMISSION PREVENTIVE	PROCES/ PRODUCT REDESIGN MATERIAL CHOICE	NEW SYSTEMS FOR FUNCTIONS AND NEEDS

Systems Renewal

The trajectories of System Optimisation and of System Improvement are well covered by actual policies and policy instruments. The challenge now is to initiate a process of Systems Renewal.

The "future generations- concept" implies the necessity of Systems Renewal within 20–50 years. To develope fundamental system renewal takes several decades of time from "concept to market". These terms of time go far beyond the terms which are usual in business. Initiation of processes of Systems Renewal has then, given the characteristics of the processes, to cope with new questions and dilemmas such as:
- Handling uncertainties on long term trends and risks, including different risk perceptions based on different appreciation of normative and scientific analyses and future expectations (WRR 1994).
- New roles and forms of co-operation between market, science & technology and government and NGO's taking their specific strengths, weaknesses and responsibilities into account.
- Involvement and participation of many actors and stake holders.
- Bridging between the drive of Competition and the necessity of Co-operation.
- Arrangements crossing (economic) sectoral borders.

In Systems Renewal all aspects of sustainability: physical, economic and social are at stake as well from a principal point of view as well as from the practical interest of viability of new means, products and processes. This requires transparency and participation in the process architecture.

What has been achieved and what still has to be achieved?

Achieved

An essential element to direct development processes is a broadly shared future orientation. Such an orientation was manifest in the post (2nd world) war period in Western Europe. The orientation was on reconstruction and rebuilding Europe. On a global scale "Our Common Future" (World Commission on Environment and Development 1987) followed by Agenda 21 served as an orientation. Unfortunately this orientation was not sufficiently concrete to initiate the necessary governmental Sustainable Development Challenges (even "Kyoto" is very modest in its ambitions as compared with the nature of the problem). In the private sphere however several actors adopted the necessity of a jump like improvement of eco-efficiency eg The WBCSD, World Business Council on Sustainable Development (WBCSD n.d.) and the "Factor 10 Institute" (Factor 10 Club 1995). The Dutch experiences learn that innovation processes opening options for radical renewal of technology systems on the long term, fitting in the process of sustainable development can be initiated and managed (Weaver et al 2000; Deutscher Bundestag 1999). Systems Innovation has been thoroughly investigated and practised by the Dutch National Council on Agricultural Research (Rutten et al 2000) and illustrates the possibility to develop shared visions and ambitions. Backcasting from need to means and from future to present proved to be a very helpful instrument. It should be noticed however that although these Dutch experiences were inspired on the basis of national policies, they still have a "stand alone" character for specific cases. This is not the case in a New Zealand foresight program (Reeve/Gandar 2000) in which a backcasting approach was followed to develop national development policies for the medium term (15 years). It also appeared to be possible to fit presentations "Towards an agenda for European Agricultural research" in a frame corresponding to the STD approach (Jansen 2000a). Organising broad co-operation through borders of economic sectors and between private parties, public parties and Science & Technology is essential to obtain sufficient commitment for long lasting viable action and research & development programs. Such co-operation is successfully organised in the UK foresight programs (Rawlins 2000) and in the Portugese program "Industria Y Tecnologi" (Gavignan 2000) and appears in almost all other projects. In Sweden a 21ste century program based on backcasting from an orientation on Sustainable Sweden is being set up (Swedish Environmental Advisory Council 2001). Altogether the conclusion is that useful experiences are gained. An undoubtedly far incomplete overview is given in the Table 4.

Table 4: Experiences in systems approach for sustainable development

			Aspect			
	Level National Gobal	Time scale	Backcasting Future to Present	Integral Need to Means	Proces	Aim
Austria Graz	N	MT	+	±	+	Regional Dev.
Netherlands (Agri)	N	MT	±	-	-	Systems. Inn.
Netherlands (STD)	N	LT	+	+	-	Sustain.Inn.
New Zealand	N	MT	+	-	+	Econ.Dev.
Portugal	N	MT	-	-	+	Econ.Dev.
Sweden	N	MT	+	-	±	Sust.Econ.Dev.
UK	N	MT	+	-	+	Econ.Dev.
WBCSD	G	MT	-	-	-	Sectoral. Dev.
WCED (Brundtland)	G	LT	+	+	+	Exploiration.
FACTOR 10 Institute	G	LT	+	+	+	Exploiration.
Natural Step	N	M & LT	+	+	-	Sust Entreprise

Education

Integration of Sustainability in education is increasingly being programmed in a number of Universities and High Schools. Examples the Association for Global Sustainability, a cooperation of – the MIT (Massachusts Institute for Technology), the ETH (Eidgenossische Technische Hochschule) in Zürich and the University of Tokyo -, another example is the Technical University of Delft in The Netherlands.

To be achieved

Start up of a process of Systems Renewal is regarded to be highly urgent. To this end the following conditions have to be fulfilled:
- Recognition by public and private parties of the necessity of development of long term societal and entrepreneurial strategies in view of "rapidly" changing conditions.
- Consistent facilitation of development of long term (± 50 years) global and robust future orientations at different levels of governmental bodies on the basis of participation.
- Indication by relevant authorities of domains of needs, fulfilling of which by means of now available and foreseen technologies will cause severe (future) ecological and social tensions at relevant regional scales.
- Development of mechanisms and instruments for co-operation between private, science & technology, NGO's and governments to develop strategies for sustainable development and to develop sustainable technologies in this frame work in combined efforts of the stake holders,
- Development of mechanisms and instruments to cover long term private economic risks and to ascertain commitment and involvement of private parties in development of new technologies.

Renewal, Improvement and Optimisation

Broadly shared future orientations serve primarily as a source for a backcasting procedure to design innovation paths for development of sustainable technologies or policy programs (Systems Renewal). Once being obtained these orientations may as well help to focus ongoing System Optimisation and System Improvement or Redesign.

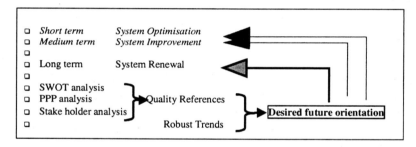

Figure 5: Long term orientation in sustainable development trajectorie.

Integral and Partial Processes, Flexibility

A heavily co-ordinated top down procedure may well result in a killing bureaucratic system. The expression "future orientation" rather than "view" or "picture" not to say "blue print" is meant to indicate that the orientation should be a rough one giving room for specific interpretations and flexible adaptation. Like the WCED report "Our Common Future" (World Commission on Environment and Development 1987) gives an orientation on development. Another illustration is the common goal in the post (2nd World) War period in Western Europe: Rebuild and Reconstruct Europe. Future orientations may well be developed top-down as well as bottom-up. Bottom-up delivers indications on the desired terms of reference for higher levels but has the disadvantage of lack of insight in the effects of neighbouring orienta-

Higher Education and Sustainable Development — 45

tions. Top-down indicates the systems borders and may be essential to overview dominant robust trends in society and governance. The conclusion is that top-down and bottom-up approaches are complimentary and may be applied without heavy formal co-ordination. Communication between relevant parties however is essential. The different levels of exploration may be regarded as a sequence of divergent and convergent processes.

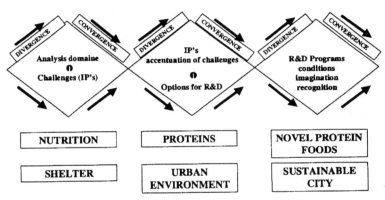

Figure 6: Divergence and Convergence in System Renewal

Relevant orientation domains are summarised in the next table:

Table 5: Application of system renewal in sustainable development

Desired Future Orientation and System Renewal		
General		
Needs	Sectors providing means	Regional
Transportation	Chemistry	Urban
Nutrition	Agriculture	Rural
Housing	Services	Integration U-R
Water	Mech. Industry	

Barriers

For a wide application of System Renewal some severe barriers have to be overcome:
- Lack of ability and/or will of private enterprises to develop strategic long term planning,
- Priority for short term profits and effects in private as well as in public,
- Lack of abilities and/or will of governmental bodies to face the consequences and impossibilities of long term continuation of traditional economic growth in view of the growing world population and over exploitation of the environment at large,
- Non eco-efficient and non-renewal approach in constructing physical infra-structural hard ware (main ports, air ports, motor ways, rail roads etc) which block development of new eco-efficient technologies and policies.
- Inherent resistance to change in large bureaucratic bodies in public and private,
- Lack of sufficient well educated change agents to act as "champions" at different levels and in different domains in private and public,
- NOT: LACK OF KNOWLEDGE AND INSIGHTS OF/IN NECESSARY STEPS, PROCESSES, (POLICY) INSTRUMENTS. THESE ARE SUPERFLUOUS AVAILABLE.

Dilemma's

- Process and Products.
  A draw back of Systems Renewal is that it requires a continuous process in a direction given by terms of reference. Decision makers who have to invest in this process usually demand a concrete and recognisable description of the result of the process to defend their interest in it. Especially in the first phases of development on the other hand, fixation on a too concrete model or goal for the outcome of the process may well block the creativity in develop-

ing new options. This makes funding of these phases which are essential to obtain new options, to a hard job.
- Disciplinary status « transdisciplinary effectiveness.
Systems Renewal requires fusion of knowledge between disciplines, sectors and institutions. At the same time the status of interdisciplinary work is still low in scientific publications and in peer evaluations in funding procedures research programs.
- Political competencies ↔ Formal representation democracy « Participation.
In the existing political cultures tensions may arise between participation and formal democratic institutions. In participatory processes governors may accept obligations to the participating parties. In the set-up of a future orientation, for example, the government should oblige itself to facilitate the set-up without claiming more influence than other participating partners. In the political arena however the governor has to defend the result exclusively from his point of view. A situation in which representatives – without having participated in the process – demand conflicting changes of the outcome could be destructive.

Systems Renewal in Governmental Practises

Sustainability oriented governmental policies pointing to Systems Renewal differ essentially from more traditional environmental policies pointing to Systems Optimisation and Systems Improvement. The degree of uncertainty, the scope of action, the accentuation in the sequence from production process to need fulfilment result in essentially differing driving forces and effect of administrative incentives imply a different role and attitude from Government.

As compared with System Optimisation and System Improvement, the process of System Renewal is charactarised by a long time scale, a high rate of uncertainties, a high complexity, involvement of many actors and strong interaction "culture-structure –technology".

Consequently this requires different approaches of government in shaping conditions for sustainable development.

Table 6 : Characteristics of technological development trajectories

TRACKS FOR DEVELOPMENT	OPTIMISATION	ADAPTION, IMPROVEMENT AND REDESIGN		RENEWAL
		END OF PROCESS END OF PRODUCT	INTEGRATED IN PROCESS/PRODUCT	
INNOVATION TYPE	Incremental	Incremental	Radical	New Systems Paradigm Shift
NATURE OF CHALLENGE / MANAGERIAL LEVEL	Operational Factory	Implementational Division		Conceptual Company
DRIVING FORCES	Real costs Savings Public Image	→		Believes in LT – dev. shared prospects
ADMINISTRATIVE INCENTIVES	Regulation	Regulation Fin.Support	MT Standards Taxation Sectoral Agreements	Strategical Development Cooperation
DEGREE OF UNCERTAINTY	Low	Low	Moderate	High
SCOPE OF ACTION	Micro	Micro	Meso Intrasectoral	Macro Intersectoral
SPECIFICATION LEVEL	Process	Process / Materials	Materials / Product / Function	Function / Need
MOST RELEVANT ACTORS	Private Enterprise	Private Enterprise	Private Enterprise / Techn. Institutes	University / Techn. Institute / Private Enterprise

Technology forcing by setting (future) standards may lead to Systems Optimisation and Improvement up to middle long terms, it will not evoke private parties to undertake the risky development of System Renewal. Government can forbid private parties to act irresponsible but not command to take future risks of development.

Higher Education and Sustainable Development — 49

Against this background governmental parties have to play an active role in copyingnew questions and dilemmas, as mentioned in § 3.

This requires a changing and active role of government with respect to:
- Taking responsibility for development of shared future orientations, as a basis to set up Long Term System Renewal programs,
- Risk sharing with private parties and Science and Technology in Long Term System Renewal development programs,

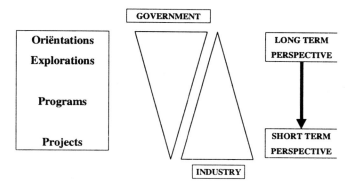

Figure 7: *Public and Private funding of Systems Renewal*

- Participation in and organising of Co-operation between relevant stake holders and
- Develop structures and opportunities for Participation of non industrial stake holders.

Meeting these demands requires a change in governmental attitude and structures in New Public Management: The Enterprising Government (Bemelmans et al 1999). In time and intensity these changes may run parallel to the subsequent changes in Systems from optimisation on the short term up to Renewal at the long term.

Proposals

The ambition

The ambition is to handle the tension between the urgency to renew numerous systems to fulfil peoples needs and the inertia of processes of fundamental change. On the one hand overacting and neglecting the inertia of change may produce counter productive effects. On the other hand the pace of change has to be sufficient to achieve timely renewal of major systems.

Given the urgency and the necessary scale of Systems Renewal the proposal is to attain in the next 15 years an ongoing process of Systems Renewal in the industrialised as well as in the developing nations. In general the approach is consists of a process of interactive and iterative search in co-operative arrangements between private parties, science and technology and governmental parties taking interaction "culture - structure - technology" into account.

In the application of this approach specific national and regional cultures and traditions have to be respected.

The scale of a specific Systems Renewal process depends on the scale of the system and its effects. Top-down and bottom-up approaches will appear to be complimentary.

The COPERNICUS-Charter has to be implemented world wide within 10 years to guarantee sufficient capacity building. The experience with the embedment of SD in educational systems gained up to now should be extended and practised.

Excercising backcasting this results in step-wise approach as shown in Figure 8.

Higher Education and Sustainable Development — 51

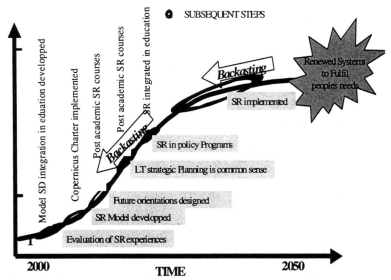

Figure 8: Governance towards Systems Renewal

The consequence is that the architecture of the Renewal process has to deliver opportunities to materialise these profits.

The steps
Ten years of experience in The Netherlands show that "learning by doing" is an effective approach to get involvement of relevant parties. In the early nineties two conditions appeared to be fulfilled to set up a program to investigate the what, how and who of Systems Renewal. At the right moment the problem window and the political window (van Gestel 1999) were both opened.

The problem window because industry and science and technology suffered from a bad image. The Sustainable Technology Development program offered the opportunity to illustrate a positive role of technology with contributing to a sustainable society.

The political window was opened because in the first Dutch National Environment Policy Plan some strategies were formulated with regard of technology. However there was no clear vision on the role of technology in the process of sustainable development. Up to then claims on (environmental) technology had a defensive and reactive nature. During the nineties the "factor X" approach has gained recognition. Analyses have shown the urgency of the question, experiments in real situations have shown the possibility and the outlook on profits of Systems Renewal. But it has become as clear that sincere efforts are necessary to get the process going.

Essentially two parallel paths have to be paved:
- Gaining experience with Systems Renewal in ever growing circles ("Stone in the pond" model) and
- Building capacity in educational systems (Ehrenfeld et al 2000).

For both paths sufficient experience exists to make a start.

The start

> Atelier to exchange national experiences with (near) System Renewal under guidance of JRC in co-operation with OECD Futures. WBCSD and the Factor 10 Institute.

To evaluate the experiences in different countries and international settings, to gain support for the ambition, and to work out a workable proposition to relevant authorities and institutions a well prepared two or three day Atelier with 30 - 50 participants may be very fruitful. The preparation could consist off bilateral communication on the experiences, on the interests of the participants and of stake holder analysis (arenas and materialised currencies) of the authorities and institutions which are supposed to play a role in the continuation.

The United Nations University of Tokyo and the Factor 10 Institute prepared and organised an International Workshop on "Synergies and Co-operation in Integrative Approaches towards Eco-Restructuring" in Carnoules (France, Provence) in June 2000. The results of the workshop publication of which is in preparation, are useful for the Atelier.

Experiences

The results of the innovation experiments result in the following indications:
- Innovation processes scooping for development of technology for a sustainable (long-term) future can be initiated and managed.
- Shared rough future orientations among relevant stakeholders are essential elements in the innovation process.
- To operationalise the essential interaction 'culture - structure - technology' requires permanent attention especially with respect to the element "culture". The nature of the operationalisation differentiates for different levels in the program from 'future visions' to 'product viability'.
- Backcasting from needs to products and from future to present is a powerful tool for creative approaches of the innovation process.
- It appears to be possible to bridge the tension between the (industrial) need for economic prospects on the medium term and the necessary orientation on long term targets for sustainability. In fact long-term envelope curves can be constructed "ex ante" covering and orienting technological development trajectories with intermediate targets and spin-offs.
- Methods have been developed to bridge the tension between the needs for broad support and for innovative creativity.
- Networks on the interfaces of different technological disciplines as well as between technological and other disciplines can be set up, maintained and operationalised.
- Investment of time in stakeholder analysis based on (bilateral) interviews is essential to create continuous support and chances for embodiment.
- Ways have been developed to approach and mobilize stakeholders in specific technology development projects.

- Ways to maintain an interactive and iterative process in innovation and decision making proved to be successful.
- Profiles for key persons (Champions) in the innovation process were established. The role of a champion is essential for a successful management of the innovation process.

References

Bemelmans, M. L. et al (1999): Renewing Government: A Tale for all Times, p. 13–34 with: Denhardt's Significance Theory on p. 30-31, in: Nelissen, N. et al, Renewing Government, Innovative and Inspiring Visions, International Books, Utrecht.

Deutscher Bundestag (1999): Drucksache 14/571/ 18.03.99, Forschungs- und Technologiepolitik für eine nachhaltige Entwicklung".

Ehrenfeld, J./Conceição, P./Heitor, M.V./Vieira, P.S. (2000): Towards Sustainable Universities: Challenges For Engineering Education In The Learning Economy, Presentation Lisbon 21-01-2000.

Factor 10 Club (1995): Carnoules Declaration, (in English, French, German, Italian, Japanese), Wuppertal Institute for Climate, Energy and Environment, Wuppertal.

Gavigan, J. (2000): Technology Foresight for Engineering and Technology in Portugal, Views from IPTS, Presentation Lisbon 21-01-2000, IPTS – Joint Research Centre, EC.

Jansen, J.L.A. (2000a): Quality of Life, Sustainable and World Wide, New Challenges for Agricultural Research, in: Boekestein, A. et al, Towards an agenda for Agricultural Research in Europe, Wageningen Pers, The Netherlands, p. 227–237.

Jansen, J.L.A. (2000b): On search for ecojumps in technology, From future visions to technology programs, in: Proceedings "Transdisciplinarity: Joint Problem Solving among Science, Technology and Society" Workbook I, Hafmans Sachbuch Verlag, Zürich Schweiz, p. 321–325.

Rawlins, D. (2000): The UK Foresight Program - Foresight for the Food Chain, in: Boekestein, A. et al, Towards an agenda for Ag-

ricultural Research in Europe, Wageningen Pers, The Netherlands, p. 85–90.
Reeve, N./Gandar, P. (2000): The New Zealand foresight project – An overview, in: Boekestein, A. et al, Towards an agenda for Agricultural Research in Europe, Wageningen Pers, The Netherlands, p. 101–110.
Rutten, H./Verkaik, A.P./de Wit, J. (2000): Using foresight to develop strategies for science technology and innovation, in: Boekestein, A. et al, Towards an agenda for Agricultural Research in Europe, Wageningen Pers, The Netherlands, p. 91–99.
Swedish Environmental Advisory Council (2001): Tänk nytt, tänk hållbart!-dialog och samverkan för hållbar utveckling (Think new, think sustainable-dialogue and cooperation for a sustainable development). To be published in march SOU 2001: 20.
van Gestel, N.M. (1999): The Right Moment for Governmental Renewal, The John. W. Kingdon's Stream Model, in: Nelissen, N. et al, Renewing Government, Innovative and Inspiring Visions, International Books, Utrecht, p. 151–169.
Vasbinder, J.W./Groen, Th. (to be published): Knowledge Valuation in PPP, A model for the valuation process in knowledge generating Public-Private-Partnerships, to be published.
WBCSD Brochure, Geneva, Business Council For Sustainable Development, World Trade Centre Building – 3rd floor –, Route de l'Aéroport 10, Geneva, Switzerland.
Weaver, P./Jansen, L./van Grootveld, G./van Spiegel, E./Vergragt, P. (2000): Sustainable Technology Development, Greenleaf Publishing, Sheffield UK.
World Commission on Environment and Development (1987): Our common future, Oxford University Press, Oxford-New York.
WRR (Scientific Council for Government Policies) (1994): Duurzame risico's: een blijvend gegeven, Sdu Uitgeverij, Den Haag.

Annex I: Steps towards System Renewal

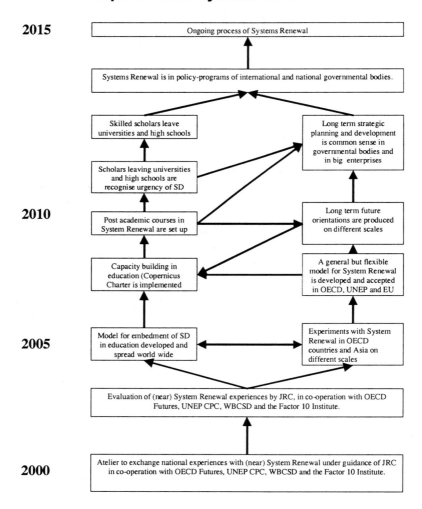

II.
Sustainability and Education

M. C. E. (Rietje) van Dam-Mieras

Reflections on Learning and Sustainable Development

Learning: a Continuing Process

Learning is a process of interaction that continues lifelong. During that process new options are tried out and continuously choices are made on which of those new options should be maintained. Two most important factors in the process are the learning individual and its learning environment. For the learner the learning process contributes to the formation of the social identity in which the individual can recognise him- or herself as a valuable individual with respect to others. The format of the learning environment depends on age, prior knowledge and social activity and therefore will continuously change during the lifelong learning process.

A classical learning route for an individual in the industrialised world could be described as follows. In early childhood a language is learned which enables communication and interaction with the social environment. After this part of the learning route the individual generally enters the educational system. It is generally agreed that an educational system that allows for efficient and effective learning is important, both from the socio-cultural and the economic perspective.

During primary and secondary education comprehension of the complex and rapidly changing culture and society grows and independent thinking is developed. During this period also the competencies to function in society are developed. After this stage the learning trajectory continues in higher or vocational education or in alternative learning environments embedded in practice. After these stages during which the learning process takes place in more or less institutionalised environments, the learning process continues and is shaped by societal functioning and personal ambitions.

In the past the social environments in which individuals grew up and functioned were relatively constant, but presently, also because of the globalisation of the economy and the rapid development of ICT, continuous change tends to be the most stable factor. The content of most professions is changing and most people must be able to integrate the use of ICT-instruments in their (professional) life (European Commission 2000). Furthermore people should be able to reflect critically on information, should develop good social competencies, both normative and communicative, and should be able to work in multi-disciplinary teams on complex problems (Gibbons et al. 1994, 1998). Of course such changes should also be reflected in the institutionalised learning opportunities within the educational system. A continuously changing society asks for a responsive educational system doing justice to differences in talents and in social, economic and cultural backgrounds. Individual learning environments should become more dynamic and individualised on the one hand and introduce the international aspects of economic globalisation and its consequences on the other. The use of ICT-tools in the design and development of learning environments can be most promising, both for individualising a learning environment and for creating the possibility to develop worldwide co-operative learning processes; both are needed.

Of course the foregoing is a description of education in those parts of the world where most individuals follow a shorter or longer trajectory in an educational system. There are also parts of the world, however, where such a learning route is less obvious. In those parts of the world the learning process in early childhood is the same, but after that period the learning process is only embedded in a practice that consists of a continuous struggle for the basic needs to stay alive. Also those learning environments should be changed but that challenge is so much more demanding than that in countries belonging to the former category.

Education: Creating Conditions to Learn

Education could be described as a institutionalised process aimed at realising defined learning objectives for defined target groups. The learning objectives comprise disciplinary, social, cultural, and economic items. The target groups can be divided according to age and the level of prior education or development. The educational system tries to provide contexts which support the learning of individuals. Starting from theoretical concepts of learning it is tried to create a set of conditions favouring the individual learning processes. The learning environment is designed, the content is structured, the learning process is supervised and the results are tested.

Traditionally learning facts gets much emphasis in education, which is in agreement with the classical ideals of erudition and scholarship. In this classical approach ordering of knowledge within specific domains plays an important role. The objectives of the learning process are often described starting from these disciplines. An analysis of the objectives must give insight in the optimal conditions to realise the learning objectives. This approach can be effective in domains that are characterised by independent learning objectives, but is less satisfying in situations characterised by a more integrated and complex sets of learning objectives. For the didactic design of learning environments a starting point in a specific discipline mostly implies a learning process in a relatively closed system. For the learner it means that the formal learning process takes place in a learning environment that is relatively shielded from society and that the application of knowledge in vocational or societal practice only occurs after the formal learning process has finished.

Presently a shift from an emphasis on learning facts to an emphasis on developing competencies can be observed in many countries. Most probably acquiring knowledge will remain an important objective, but the possibility to actively manipulate knowledge within a practical context becomes more important. This implies that knowledge must continuously be translated to specific contexts and specific target groups. For the didactic model this means more emphasis on an active, individualised learning process in a rich, complex and more open learning environment. This type of learning must prepare individuals for functioning in complex professional or societal settings in which they will be confronted with multidisciplinary approaches of complex problems and will have to work together with experts from different disciplinary domains. In comparison with traditional education, mainly focussed on the acquisition of knowledge, competences oriented education gives much more attention to role playing, tasks and problem solving (Kerka 1997, Lynch 1997, van Loo en Semeijn 2000, Kreijns et al 2001, Westera et al. 2001).

A rich and complex learning environment can be embedded in the infrastructure of a school or a university, but can also be (partly) embedded in vocational life situations. While working on authentic tasks the learning individual produces a mental model, which is a representation of reality. Such models can be used to explore the 'real world', to explain, forecast and draw conclusions. The validity of such mental models is continuously tested during interactions with the physical and social environment. In the social environment opinions are formed during interactions with other individuals each having their own perspective on reality. An authentic learning environment not only offers the opportunity of interaction with the physical and social environment, it also supports orientation on the problems met in practice. A problem orientation during the learning process contributes to bridging the gap between the development of knowledge and the application of knowledge.

What the optimal learning environment looks like will of course depend on the specific learning objective and the specific target group. Generally speaking, however, in many western countries a gradual shift from a behavioristic to a cognistivistic oriented approach of learning is observed in the literature on learning theory. In parallel a shift from a teacher oriented to a learner oriented approach is found in the literature on teaching. In agreement with these shifts an increasing interest in the development of competencies and in working and learning in multidisciplinary teams is found. The latter can be seen as a parallel to the shift from mode 1 to mode 2 knowledge as described by Gibbons (Gibbons 1994, 1998).

Education and Sustainability

In the preceding section some reflections on learning and on the educational system are given. The perspective from which they are given is typically that of those parts of the world were educational systems are well developed. The driving force behind their development mostly has been their socio-cultural and economic relevance as perceived by national governance structures. The underlying objective has been to develop an effective and efficient system for the transfer of knowledge to and in society.

In industrialised countries the educational systems certainly have greatly contributed to economic growth. From the point of view of the industrialised world economic growth has both positive and negative aspects. On the one hand, economic development has made possible the complex and energy-intensive structures underlying the technology based lifestyles in that part of the world. On the other hand those developments are paid for by a growing tension between human production- and consumption sysems and the ecological sustainability of System Earth (Ayres 1998, Barbiroli 1996, Røpke 2001, van Dam-Mieras et al. 1996, Simonis 1994, Weaver et al., 2000). The challenge is to realise a development process that does justice to both ecological sustainability and economic growth on a worldwide scale. Against this background the question whether the educational system is still effective and efficient in a world that is continuously changing among others by globalisation of the economy, is very relevant. With respect to the aspect of global social equity this question can not only be asked on a national level.

As the future remains unpredictable, continuous change implies a greater responsiveness and flexibility of the educational system. This in turn means that, in order to accommodate that flexibility and allow for experiments, the educational system has to reflect on values that can be used as anchoring points for development. In western societies such anchoring points are the normative values such as freedom, personal development, equity, social integration and stability which are considered to be critical for the civil society (WRR 2002). Until now in most countries sustainable development is not among those anchoring points, in spite of the fact that history has shown that societies with sufficient social cohesion, knowledge and capital have great flexibility and capacity to survive and that responsible management of natural resources is of utmost importance in this respect (Cohen 1997, Rotmans en de Vries 1997). Lubchenko (Lubchenko 1998) states that '*The new and unmet needs of society include more comprehensive information, understanding, and technologies for society to move towards a more sustainable biosphere – one which is ecologically sound, economically feasible, and socially just. New fundamental research, faster and more effective transmission of new and existing knowledge to policy- and decision-makers, and better communication of this knowledge to the public will all be required to meet this challenge*'. Indeed these conditions will have to be met if we want to realise a more sustainable future, but one might feel that the statement is perhaps too optimistic about what could be achieved by technology. Perhaps much more emphasis should be given to normative political choices for more social equity in a global economy. As stated above, a more sustainable development must reconcile ecological sustainability with economic growth and of course the creation of knowledge, its transfer to society and its application in technology are very important in this respect, but what is also very important is the choice for social equity in a global perspective.

A more sustainable development is important for all sectors of society. The growth of the world population, of the economy, the globalisation of agricultural and industrial production and of he service sector all contribute to stress on the environment. Problems in the domain of sustainable development are complex problems in which norms and values of different stakeholders, scientific knowledge, uncertainty and dealing with risks all play a role. They ask for a multidisciplinary approach in which the different stakeholders (companies, government, NGO's, citizens) work together.

Education forms part of the infrastructure that prepares individuals for, and supports them during, their functioning in society. As stated above, individuals should not only learn facts, they should also be given the opportunity to develop competencies (cognitive, meta-cognitive, social, affective). Because sustainable development can be considered as a very important concept for the future of Mankind, the concept deserves attention in the learning path of all individuals. According to educational specialists effective and efficient learning processes ask for rich and complex authentic learning environments; sustainable development an its global dimensions certainly must be part of those environments.

Education and ICT: Tools to Support Learning

From the preceding paragraphs it can be concluded that the challenge of sustainable development, reconciling ecological sustainability with economic growth, requires that not only the economy, but also its effects on ecological systems and social equity, should be seen from a global perspective. Both this global perspective and the rapid changes caused by globalisation and ICT-development should get a place in the learning environment of all individuals. Of course the choice for specific development strategies and for more global social equity remains a normative political choice of governments and companies, but individual citizens should at least have a chance to learn about different options for a more sustainable development during education. As learning asks for a continuous interaction with physical and social environments, creative solutions have tot be found to introduce the global dimension in the learning environment of individuals. ICT-tools could be very useful for that purpose.

ICT-tools can indeed be used to support learning. They can be used to structure contents, to support routine tasks, to support the development of competencies, to monitor the results of the learning process, and to increase the degrees of freedom in time, space and pace of learning. To realize these opportunities human creativity and teamwork are of great importance. For the effective use of ICT-tools in the learning process they must constitute an integrated part of the learning environment, which asks for a didactic starting point in the design and development of those environments (Rocha Trindade et al., 1998, Mioduser and Nachmias 1999, Kreijns et al. 2001, Westera et al. 2001).

The ways ICT-tools are used in education reflect the different theoretical perspectives on learning.

According to the behavioristic approach learning takes place via the confirmation of a reaction of the learner to a stimulus and during learning independent units of information are added to pre-existing knowledge. This approach leads to computer supported learning during which the learner follows a strongly guided trajectory of interaction with computer software. The ICT-products are courseware, drill and practice exercises and tutorials.

According to the cognitivistic approach the processing of mental models by the learner during its confrontation with new information is of crucial importance. The new information must be actively integrated into the pre-existing knowledge. Within this cognitivistic theory constructivism assumes that individuals construct their own knowledge and that the learner always is interpreting information from the personal knowledge situation. Information is not stored in the way it is offered, but it is actively reconstructed from personal and context dependent insights; in this way the learner constructs its own knowledge. Social interactions during learning process offer possibilities for making knowledge explicit, for reflection on insights, strategies, ways of thinking and methods of problem solving. Problem orientation during learning can be seen as a stimulus for the learning process. The constructivistic approach leads to information rich environments in which learners interact with each other and with tutors while working on authentic tasks. The use of groupware can support the learning process by enabling time and place independent forms of co-operative learning. In principle electronic learning environments are flexible and consist of a content part, a communication part, and a managerial part. The practical experience with electronic learning environments is still rather limited, but the level of interactivity seems to be a critical success factor (Urban 2000, Graves 2001, Eurelings et al. 2002).

The importance of social interaction during the learning process was stressed by the MIT President in relation to the free access via internet to all MIT content, course materials and video's of MIT in the following way (Richards 2001): *'Let me be clear: We are not providing a MIT education on the Web. We are providing our core materials that are the infrastructure that undergrids an MIT education. Real education requires interaction, the interaction is part of American teaching. We think that OpenCourseWare will make it possible for faculty to concentrate even more on the actual interactions between faculty and students that are the real core of learning'.*

Until now the rather limited amount of experience available makes clear that electronically supported co-operative learning offers good opportunities for the development of basic skills and more general competencies. For a meaningful use of ICT-tools to support social interaction in the learning environment the conditions for co-operation must constitute an explicit part of its didactic design. Just as face to face teamwork, electronically supported teamwork depends on the development of trust between team members and their active participation in the process. A social interaction component in processes of co-operative learning is based on interactivity between team members and this involves both informal chatting and task oriented discussions. The social interaction must be deliberately incorporated and methods must be developed to instrument, encourage and facilitate it. The chances for failure are more in the social than in the technological domain (Kreijns et al 2001.).

The (re)design of learning environments can have far reaching consequences for both learners and teachers. The use of ICT-tools in learning environments asks for teamwork in all stages of their design, development and application. In the development team didactic knowledge, technological knowledge, domain specific scientific knowledge and experience in teaching must be integrated. During the development stage knowledge and experience from teaching practice must be available for designers and in later stages the experiences of users must be used for improving the design. Also the use of ICT-supported learning environments in teaching practice asks for cooperation between teachers and ICT-specialists to prevent that ICT-tools become frustrating instead of facilitating.

Again this section describes developments taking place in the industrialised world where in general an educational system is considered to be relevant for social and economic developments. In those countries nowadays both education and lifelong learning are considered to be important for the continuous development of a knowledge based economy. The use of ICT-tools can certainly contribute to innovation of the educational performance in that part of the world. If we should feel that the rapid developments in the field of ICT should not enlarge the existing gap between the industrialised part of the world and the so called developing part of the world, we should find ways to share knowledge and experiences in a more global learning environment. And for this to become reality not only individuals must learn, but the different societies as well. Also here the social and political hurdles most probably will be turn out to be more insurmountable than the technological ones. Do we let this happen?

References

Ayres, R. (1998): Ecorestructuring: the transition to an ecologically sustainable economy, in: Ayres, R./Weaver, P. (eds.), Ecorestructuring: implications for sustainable development, Tokyo, United Nations University Press.

Barbiroli, G. (1996): The role of technology and science in sustainable development, in: Nath, B./Hens, L./Devuyst, D. (eds.), Sustainable Development, VUBPRESS, Brussels.

Cohen, J. M. (1997): Risk and Ecological modernisation, Futures, 29, 105.

Dam-Mieras, M.C.E. van/Mijnbeek, G./Middelbeek, E. (1996): Biotechnology applications in an environmental perspective, in: Mistra, K.B. (ed.), Clean Production, environmental and economic perspectives, Springer-Verlag, Berlin.

Eurelings, A.M.C./Melief, A.B.M./Plekkenpol, H. (2001): Leren in een kennissamenleving. De gevolgen van de digitale revolutie voor het hoger onderwijs en de beroeps- en volwassenmeneducatie in Nederland, Sdu Uitgevers, Den Haag.

European Commission (2000): Designing Tomorrow's Education Promoting Innovation with New Technologies (COM(2000) 23), Commission of the European Communities, Brussels.

Gibbons, M. (1998): Higher Education Relevance in the 21st Century, UNESCO World Conference on Higher Education, Paris, October 5–9.

Gibbons, M./Limoges, C./Nowotny, H./Schwartzmann, S./Scott, P./Trow, M. (1994): The new Production of Knowledge, Sage, London.

Graves, W.H. (2001): Virtual operations, EDUCAUSE review, march/april.
Kerka, S. (1997): Constructivism, workplace learning and vocational education, ERIC Digest.
Kreijns, K./Kirschner, P. A./Jochems, W. (2001): The sociability of computer-supported collaborative learning environments.
Loo, J. van/Semeijn, J. (2000): Measuring competencies in schoolleaver surveys, paper presented at the 5th Annual ILM Conference, Aberdeen, Scotland.
Lynch, R. L. (1997): Designing vocational and technical teacher education for the 21^e century, ERIC Clearing House.
Mioduser, D./Nachmias, R. (1999): Web-based learning environments, current implementation and evolving trends, Tel-Aviv University.
Richards, P. (2001): MIT to make nearly all course materials available free on the World Wide Web, MIT news, April 4.
Rocha Trindade, A./Carette-d'Haucourt, F./van Dam-Mieras, R./ arinetti, L./ Johnsen, B./Larsen, S./Lorentsen, A./Peraya, D./Percy, K./Sundin, B. (1998): Trends in open and distance education. A review and recommendations. Conference of European Union Rectors'Conferences, Working group on open and distance learning, Lisbon.
Røpke, I. (2001): New technology in everyday life - social processes and environmental impact, Ecological Economics, 38, 403–422.
Rotmans, J./en de Vries, B. (1997): Perspectives on global change – the TARGETS approach, Cambridge University Press, Cambridge.
Simonis, U. (1994): Industrial restructuring in industrial countries, in: Ayres R./Simonis, U. (eds.), Industrial metabolism: restructuring for sustainable development, United Nations Press, Tokyo.
Urban, T. (2000): Success criteria for e-learning operations, Red Herring.
Westera, W./Sloep, P. B./Gerissen, J.F. (2000): The design of the virtual company: synergism of learning and working in a net-

worked environment, Innovations in Education and Training International 37, 23-33.

WRR (2002): Van oude en nieuwe kennis, Sdu Uitgevers, Den Haag.

John Fien

Teacher Education for Sustainability: A Case Study of the UNESCO Multimedia Teacher Education Programme. Teaching and Learning for a Sustainable Future

Our Common Future, the Report of the World Commission on Environment and Development (1987) states that "the world's teachers ... have a crucial role to play" in helping to bring about "the extensive social changes" needed along the pathway towards a sustainable future (p. xiv). For teachers to play this role successfully they require a commitment to the principles of education for sustainability; without it, they may lack the insights, desire and skills to ensure that their students are provided with opportunities to learn how to contribute to the ways their communities are working to advance the transition to sustainability.

This paper develops this point about the importance of teacher education as an important element of capacity building for sustainable development. It also provides a case study of a UNESCO demonstration project that seeks to catalyse action in this area at national, regional and institutional levels. *Teaching and Learning for a Sustainable Future* is a multimedia-based teacher education programme whose 25 modules provide around 100 hours of highly interactive activities designed to enhance the teacher's understanding of sustainable development and related themes. It also develops practical skills for integrating sustainable development themes into the school curriculum, and for using the teaching methods best suited to the knowledge, values and citizenship objectives of educating for a sustainable future.

Two general points – or caveats – need to be made at the start, however. First, the literature on education for sustainability is relatively new and there has been very little explicitly written on teacher education for sustainability. Thus, it is necessary at times to draw on literature from the closely related field of environmental education. Second, much of this literature is dated and normative, i.e. it is often one or two decades old, and tends to focus on what we ought to do rather than build theory and principles upon accounts drawn from empirical research. A major reason for this may be the long-running situation in which very few teacher education courses have sought to ensure that education for sustainability and/or environmental education are embedded in the professional development experiences of teachers.

The Priority of Priorities

The international community has always had an ambitious role for teachers, perceiving them as far back as 1976 as "potentially the greatest source of educational change in an organised, orderly society" (UNESCO-UNEP 1976). Indeed, appropriate and effective teacher education is a vital first step in educating a citizenry who understands the issues and has the motivation and skills to advance the transition towards sustainability. Not surprisingly, the preparation of teachers has been described as "the priority of priorities" (UNESCO-UNEP 1990, p.1). In an early report on this theme, Wilke (1985) stated that:

> "The key to successful environmental education is the classroom teacher. If teachers do not have the knowledge, skills and commitment to environmentalise their curriculum, it is unlikely that environmentally literate students will be produced." (p.1)

The 1992 United Nations Conference on Environment and Development (UNCED) highlighted this need for teacher education. In adopting *Agenda 21*, governments committed themselves "to update or prepare strategies aimed at integrating environment and development as a cross-cutting issue into education at all levels within the next three years" (UNESCO-UNEP 1992, p.3). Chapter 36 of *Agenda 21* on 'Education, Public Awareness and Training' identified training as an important "programme area" specifically called upon educational authorities to assist the development of pre-service and in-service training programmes which address the nature and methods of education for sustainability for all teachers. Similarly, the background paper prepared for the 1997 UNESCO International Conference on Environment and Society: Education and Public Awareness for Sustainability held in Thessaloniki stressed that the messages of education for sustainability "must also be emphasised in pre-service and in-service programmes of teacher training" (UNESCO 1997, p.39). More recently, following a review of efforts to reorient around education concepts of sustainability, the Commission on Sustainable Development called for national and international action to develop guidelines for reorienting teacher education and established it as a central element of the international work plan on education for sustainability (CSD 1998, p. 8).

Despite such actions, teacher education remains a neglected aspect of element in strategies for advancing sustainability in higher education. However, it is vital to bear in mind that there are more students enrolled in teacher education programmes in the universities and colleges of the South than any other discipline or faculty. This is a reflection of the level of development and development priorities of these countries. Sadly, however, almost every single one of these teachers – as well as teacher education graduates in the North - is graduating with almost no studies in ecology, sustainable development or environmental care and without any courses preparing them to teach their pupils about sustainability in a comprehensive, holistic, values-based and action-orientated way.

Achieving such a goal requires a special commitment from teacher education institutions, a commitment that goes beyond just adding new material on sustainable development into courses. This is because education for sustainability requires a new focus and outlook within education which prospective teachers - and teacher educators - may not have experienced in their own education. This new outlook has been described as the exploration of "a new personal and individualised behaviour based on the 'global ethic' which can be realised only through the enlightenment and training of educational professionals" (Simpson et al 1988, p.17). Thus, a teacher cannot teach towards sustainability effectively solely by obtaining appropriate knowledge. Instead, Simpson et al argue that:

> *"Intensive teacher education, not merely orientation, is essential if the present fragmented approaches of traditional education are to be transcended in favour of a holistic, global approach, and inter-disciplinary and a thorough change in both the outlook and preparation of teachers and teacher educators."* (Simpson et al 1988, p.17)

Adressing a History of Neglect

However, while all seem convinced that teacher education has a major role to play in helping teachers address the imperatives of education for sustainable living, we are challenged by an international pattern of neglect in addressing this priority. A claim by Wilke, Peyton and Hungerford (1987, p. 1) that "Few, if any, teacher training programmes adequately prepare teachers to effectively achieve the goals of E.E. in their classrooms" is frequently cited in this regard. While this claim is a decade and a half old, few commentators pause to note that Hungerford and his colleagues were referring to the results a survey conducted in the mid-1970s. This neglect on *our* part may stem from a belief that little has changed since the survey over two decades ago. Certainly, a range of national and international surveys in recent years reveal important deficiencies and a lack of co-ordination in the provision of appropriate teacher education for environmental education in many parts of the world (Williams 1985, 1991; Ballantyne and Aston 1990; Spork 1992; UNESC0 and Griffith University 1993; NIER 1993, 1996; Education Network for Environment and Development n.d.).

Fortunately, several projects that address the 'priority of priorities' are being developed in various parts of the world. Examples include:
- the *Toolbox* in-service education project conducted by the National Consortium for Environmental Education and Training in the United States (Monroe et al 1993);
- diverse initiatives in the United Kingdom sponsored by WWF, Forum for the Future and the UK Panel on Sustainable Development and several local education authorities (eg Bullock et al 1996);
- the Environmental Education Initiative in Teacher Education in Europe (Brinkman and Scott, 1994, 1996);
- the UNESCO Learning for a Sustainable Environment: Innovation in Teacher Education project in Asia and the Pacific (UNESCO-ACEID, 1994; Fien, Heck and Ferreira, 1997; Fien, Kumar and Ravindranath, forthcoming);
- a professional development programme for over 70 teacher education colleges in the province of Karnataka in India;
- a network of teacher education and resource centres in China sponsored by WWF (WWF 1999);
- a national teacher education programme in New Zealand that has trained over 40 people to provide in-service training for teachers in their local regions;
- a national teacher education programme in South Africa that has appointed a coordinator in each province, established a range of curriculum and resource development projects, and is developing a national structure for the accreditation of teachers who complete the courses (van Rensburg and Lotz 2000); and
- a UNESCO Chair for the Reorientation of Teacher Training to Address Sustainability at York University (Canada).

The impacts of programmes such as these are yet to be analysed. However, the barriers to teacher and school change are great, as noted by Fensham when he wrote of one of these projects:

"Invitations to change, or to try innovatory teaching strategies are almost inevitably seen as 'additions' and hence requiring extra time and effort. The suggestion to innovate often comes as part of an external innovator's timetable and not, at the point in the teachers' lives when they are dissatisfied with their present practice, and hence are looking for alternatives to solve a problem they personally recognise. The uncertain outcomes of using alternative pedagogies also are more likely to be seen as threatening the teacher's authority and stability of their classrooms than as improving these relationships, as they may in fact do." (UNESCO-ACEI, 1994)

Such issues provides the background against which teacher education for sustainability needs to be seen. They also highlight the difficulties faced by teacher educators who have most often been trained in single disciplines, and do not usually see their disciplines contributing to education for sustainability - even when they are biology or geography teachers - and who are unfamiliar with interdisciplinary teaching and the student-centred teaching methods that are best able to develop the ethical, critical thinking, problem-solving and citizenship skills required for a sustainable future.

A UNESCO Demonstration Project

As part of its function as task manager for the International Work Programme on Education, Public Awareness and Training for Sustainability of the United Nations Commission on Sustainable Development, UNESCO has taken a number of initiatives to stimulate innovation and action in teacher education for sustainability. These include the UNESCO projects named in the previous section as well as sponsoring several regional conferences on the theme and an international network of over 50 universities and colleges that are collaborating with UNESCO Chair at York University. UNESCO has also sponsored a self-study professional development programme for use in pre- and in-service teacher education. Titled *Teaching and Learning for a Sustainable Future*, the programme uses multimedia technologies to provide around 100 hours of study. The multimedia format means that the programme can be accessed and used in a great many ways by teachers, student teachers and teacher educators as well as by curriculum developers, education policy makers and authors of educational materials.

The goal of *Teaching and Learning for a Sustainable Future* is to promote an holistic, interdisciplinary approach to education through which teachers can plan learning experiences that empower students to develop and evaluate alternative visions of a sustainable future and to work creatively with others to help bring their visions into effect. To achieve this goal, the objectives of the programme are:
- To develop an appreciation of the scope and purpose of educating for a sustainable future.
- To clarify concepts and themes related to sustainable development and how they can be integrated in all subject areas across the school curriculum.
- To enhance skills for integrating issues of sustainability into a range of school subjects and classroom topics.
- To enhance skills for using a wide range of interactive and learner-centred teaching and learning strategies that underpin the knowledge, critical thinking, values and citizenship objectives implicit in reorienting education towards sustainable development.
- To encourage wider awareness of available Information and Communication Technologies (ICTs), of the potential of multimedia-based approaches to education and professional development and of the Internet as a rich source of educational materials.
- To enhance skills in computer literacy and multimedia education.

These objectives are integrated throughout the 25 modules in *Teaching and Learning for a Sustainable Future*. Figure 1 is a list of the titles of these modules and the four thematic categories into which they are organised.

Curriculum Rationale	Teaching about Sustainability Across the Curriculum
1. Exploring global realities 2. Understanding sustainable development 3. A futures perspective in the curriculum 4. Reorienting education for a sustainable future 5. Accepting the challenge	6. Sustainable futures across the curriculum 7. Citizenship education 8. Health education 9. Consumer education
Interdisciplinary Curriculum Themes	Teaching and Learning Strategies
10. Culture and religion for a sustainable future 11. Indigenous knowledge and sustainability 12. Women and sustainable development 13. Population and development 14. Understanding world hunger 15. Sustainable agriculture 16. Sustainable tourism 17. Sustainable communities	18. Experiential learning 19. Story-telling 20. Values education 21. Enquiry learning 22. Appropriate assessment 23. Future problem-solving 24. Learning outside the classroom 25. Community problem solving

Figure 1: The 25 modules in Teaching and Learning for a Sustainable Future

It is not intended that *Teaching and Learning for a Sustainable Future* be used in its published form. Rather, UNESCO has developed the programme as a demonstration project to illustrate:

1. **Ways of meeting the professional development needs of educating for a sustainable future.** For example:
   - How interdisciplinary approaches can be applied in education in order to better understand the interconnectedness of life and the complexity of the problems of the planet.
   - How to combine training about sustainable development issues with training in how to teach about them.
   - How to deal with the values laden nature of sustainable development issues in an educationally worthwhile and professionally ethical manner.
   - How to encourage ongoing reflection (via a learning journal) as a key aspect of on-going professional development.

2. **The potential of international collaboration in providing resources for teacher professional development.** For example:
   - How an international organisation such as UNESCO can establish a collaborative framework for the planning, development,

trial, revision and distribution of educational materials in a way that provides for wide international consultation and input, flexibility of design, ongoing evaluation and review, and wide institutional, national and international support.
- How the various sectors and elements of a large and diverse organisation such as UNESCO can contribute to a common programme.
- How the resources of numerous international organisations - within the United Nations family, international agencies, ministries of education, teachers' unions and non-government organisations - can be integrated into a successful and resource-rich partnership for educational change.

3. **The potential uses and benefits of multimedia technologies in pre- and in-service teacher education.** For example:
   - How multimedia approaches can be used to provide professional development experiences for a wide range of educators at various phases of their professional career.
   - How a professional development resource may be prepared to allow maximum flexibility for individual and small group use.
   - How such flexibility can allow for the use of the multimedia resource for both independent study and use as part of a tertiary course.
   - How capacity building in the use of Information and Communication Technology (ICT) can be enhanced as a 'by-product' of professional development in other fields.
   - How the scale of impact of a programme may be maximised for a large audience (60 million teachers) through the effective use of ICT and innovative multimedia design.

UNESCO was conscious that, as a demonstration project, *Teaching and Learning for a Sustainable Future* needed to be designed to allow maximum flexibility for those who might want to adapt or otherwise modify the programme. Examples of flexibility that are integrated into the design of the programme include:

Diverse audiences
The programme has been designed for both pre-service teacher education, ie for student teachers, and in the in-service-education of experienced teachers. At the same time, it has also been designed to suit the professional development needs of curriculum developers, education policy makers and authors of educational materials also.

Choice of formats
The programme is available in two multimedia formats – on the Internet at <www.unesco.org/education/tlsf> and as a CD-ROM. The CD-ROM contains the entire website, complete with over 500 Internet links that can be accessed directly from the CD-ROM (via an Internet connection). A separate PDF files of every module is also provided to enable printing and use of the programme in 'hard copy' format – although, of course, the multimedia interactions will not work in this format.

Choice of activities
Each of the 25 modules is divided into 5 to 7 activities with each one usually taking between 30 and 40 minutes. The personal Learning Journal integrated into the programme means that busy users can 'save' their work after one or two activities and come back to the module when they have more time. All of the activities can also be studied independently and can be accessed to obtain specific information via a 'Search' function.

Simplicity of design
The visual design of *Teaching and Learning for a Sustainable Future* provides an attractive learning environment and is based upon an attractive range of colours and icons. However, the design has been kept simple and is free of the large files and complex graphics that increase donwload time and costs. This also means that the programme can operate on a computer with a relatively simple hardware specification.

Learning styles
The many different types of professional development activities integrated into *Teaching and Learning for a Sustainable Future* provide a rich variety of learning experiences that cater for many learning styles.

Large sections of text have been kept to a minimum – and then are mostly located in pop-up boxes for users to read when they are ready or even print out to read at a later time. Instead, information is provided in a variety of forms (eg text, tables, diagrams, audio-files and linked Internet-sites). The activities require users to analyse and interpret this information and to apply the ideas learnt to local curriculum and teaching contexts. A Learning Journal allows users to summarise questions, answers and reflections and save them in a word processing programme.

Adaptable
The 'open architecture' used to create the files in *Teaching and Learning for a Sustainable Future* means that the programme can be easily adapted and translated for different educational and cultural contexts.

Multimedia technologies provided the key to ensuring such flexibility. Thus, the multimedia approach to the design and delivery of the programme was not chosen because it is a modern trend or fad. Indeed, UNESCO is very conscious of the 'digital divide' and the problems of access to computers and the internet in many parts of the world. However, the advantages of multimedia approaches, on balance, outweighed these concerns. For example, multimedia products such as web-sites and CD-ROMs, are very inexpensive to produce and distribute and can be accessed in most teacher education institutions in the South, even if such technologies are not widely available elsewhere in a country. Educationally, multimedia-based learning has the potential to be highly interactive and is capable of supporting the experiential learning based pedagogy that underpins the development of understanding, reflection and application processes hat underlie reflection-in-action in professional development (Schon 1983; Hart 1990). Also, multimedia products can be easily adapted and translated to suit the educational and cultural contexts of different countries.

To ensure that he programme was suitable for adaptation in many different national and regional contexts, several levels of consultation were developed. The Centre for Innovation and Research in Environmental Education at Griffith University, Australia, prepared the original drafts of the materials using resources from UNESCO and other international organisations as starting points. An international reference group and over 50 Programme Specialists within UNESCO advised on the text and pedagogical approaches used in the programme. These steps sought to ensure that Version 1 of the programme was educationally sound, accurate and up-to-date, fair in its treatment of issues, and culturally appropriate for use in international settings. The programme was also featured in many workshops and conferences during this development phase and the comments of participants integrated into the programme as it was being prepared.

Version 1 was published in January 2001 and was the focus of an extensive international evaluation by several hundred teachers and educators, sustainable development experts and multimedia specialists. These were provided by organisations such as UNESCO field offices, members of the UNESCO Associated Schools Project, UNESCO Clubs, the International Network for the Reorientation of Teacher Training to Address Sustainability managed by the UNESCO Chair at York University (Canada), the International Baccalaureate Organisation, Education International and the World Confederation of Teachers. This evaluation process identified many valuable features in Version 1 (see Figure 2) as well as areas where improvements could be made and the quality of the programme improved. These suggestions by the reviewers on all these points were integrated into the current version of the programme (Version 2).

Sustainability and Education

Australia
The themes in the modules are very interesting, but become even more attractive and enjoyable to study because of the way in which they are presented and because they are combined with practical activities and concrete examples from the field. It is captivating and easy to understand. Concepts can be incorporated easily as they are cross-curricular. It is a valuable resource for teachers and students.

Canada
After having studied this programme my own perspective has been expanded and challenged. I believe that I have gained a more global view of reorienting education for a sustainable future. I now have a better appreciation for reorienting education in other areas of the world. The presented themes in the modules are very interesting, but became even more attractive and enjoyable to study because of the way in which they are presented and because they are combined with practical activities and concrete examples from the field. I found the activities to have a lot of enrichment and alternatives for individual expression. For example, the links to other web sites as well as the references are extremely useful as an extension of the core activities. I found myself venturing to other sites to learn more about specific topics that I was personally interested in finding out about in more detail.

China
In my country, more and more people pay much attention to sustainable development, but there are few materials and resources, so I think this programme will be very helpful. And it will be significant to use it especially in pre-service teacher training institutions.

Costa Rica
It provides a sense that there is a global movement to foster a new kind of citizenship that goes beyond traditional nation-state approaches. It is a good way of conveying information, stimulating interaction and experiencing the connectivity to a global network of concerned educators.

India
Very timely. In India, concerted efforts have been made by certain organisations to re-orient education for sustainability. In this context, this UNESCO programme will be of great relevance. It is informative, well written. It is a highly informative, richly referenced and is a very good teaching-learning experience. It is a user-friendly package and the instructions are clear. Hence there was no difficulty in using and learning from the package. It combines graphics, sound and text, with web connections. Instructions and navigation are excellent. A good learning experience. It is not an exaggeration to say that each module is comprehensive and motivates one to read the next module. The titles are very attractive and catchy.

Nicaragua
The topics and issues covered in the CD ROM are of the utmost importance for the present and future of all humanity, and thus it is necessary that these values and practices are communicated to the children and young people of today's world, because they are not only the future, but also the present. I am taking some of the teaching elements of Module 7 to work at a community level, teaching local leaders and youth on civil society participatory processes.

Nigeria
All the modules are relevant to our circumstances in Nigeria and could be beneficial. It is both interesting and challenging. Its interactive nature makes for active learning. It provides great insight into the population, environment and development nexus. I intend to incorporate some of the concepts and issues into our teacher education programme in my university. It is very interactive and therefore engages the learner actively. Very interactive and exciting. It also enhanced my computer literacy skills.

Spain
The program develops innovative educational approaches in support of sustainable development by enabling teachers to learn more about holistic, interdisciplinary approaches and acquire new professional skills, especially in using multimedia resources.

South Africa
I have been grappling with these issues for many years. It was wonderful to see that it has all been pulled together in such a broad, systematic, inspiring and practical way. The programme gives clear and detailed information on setting up the computer and using the programme. For example, guidance is given on the themes and modules and what they comprise, on the use of the navigation bar, on the use of the Journal, visiting Internet sites, pop-up windows, the glossary, etc.

Thailand
It provided an excellent model for inquiry based learning. Experiencing the learning activities ourselves led to a lot of discussion, information processing, and making generalisations. It was good to experience first hand the kinds of things we ask of our students. It helped us to reflect upon our own understandings and classroom practice.

United Kingdom
It's an impressive piece of work and brings together a lot of disparate sources into one place ... It has authority, and should help the reorientation process that it seeks to assist. Quite easy to navigate and is well and attractively designed. ... a significant and important resource.

Uzbekistan
The programme develops innovative educational approaches in support of sustainable development by enabling teachers to learn more about holistic, interdisciplinary approaches and acquire new professional skills, especially in using multimedia resources. As schoolteachers, we can say that this programme is very valuable and complete. We discovered a lot of innovations, new teaching methods and new methods of presentation of information that were not known to us before.

Figure 2: Comments from the international review of Version 1

Using Teaching and Learning for a Sustainable Future

The flexibility of sue and access provided by the multimedia format of *Teaching and Learning for a Sustainable Future* means that the programme can be sued in many different ways, either by teachers independently or by teacher educators as part of a course.

Independent Learning

Individuals and small groups of teachers can study the programme independently, either from the Internet or a CD-ROM in their own time, either at work or at home. This means that teachers no longer have to wait for a workshop or training seminar to be organised in their schools or districts. This has often been a problem for teachers in the past, especially for those that teach in remote locations. The modules and activities can be studied in any order – and can be studied either alone or in small staffroom or study groups, even in remote areas. The opportunity to study anywhere, anytime provided by multimedia means that teachers, can plan their own professional development and study topics of their choice in their own time. The sense of independence and responsibility that this brings can bring a new professionalism to teaching and, thus, help raise the status of teachers.

The personalised Learning Journal means that multiple users can work from the one CD-ROM or Internet-linked computer but with a high level of confidentiality for the Learning Journal files of individuals. This is because Learning Journals, when opened, are automatically downloaded onto the hard drive of the computer or a floppy disk to be saved as a word processing file. Learning Journal files can even be printed out, completed by hand, and stored as a set of paper files in a folder.

Opportunities in Teacher Education Courses

Professors, lecturers and others responsible for developing teacher education curricula will find many opportunities for using *Teaching and Learning for a Sustainable Future* in their courses. UNESCO grants permission to teacher education institutions to load a copy of *Teaching and Learning for a Sustainable Future* on a local server (to reduce access and download time for staff and students) and to duplicate copies of the CD-ROM for free distribution to their students.

Teaching and Learning for a Sustainable Future can be used in a teacher education programme in a variety of ways: Sample course outlines are provided in the programme to illustrate:

- A stand-alone course on Teaching and Learning for a Sustainable Future,
- a selection of modules integrated into a stand-alone course on a specific education topic,
- a selection of modules integrated into other courses on specific education topics as enrichment material.

In all of these cases, *Teaching and Learning for a Sustainable Future* can be studied on-line or from the CD-ROM – in class-time, as pre- or post-class activities, or as a full e-learning experience.

Adapting and Translating the Programme

National and regional adaptations and translations of *Teaching and Learning for a Sustainable Future* are encouraged with UNESCO is ready to work with government ministries, regional organisations, teacher education institutions and others responsible for the professional development of teachers to help facilitate these changes.

Many types of adaptation are possible, from minor wording changes in the webpages and learning journal, to major changes to the number and sequence of activities and modules.

Basic adaptations involve changes to the webpages (including pop-up boxes) and learning journal. The types of text changes that could be considered include, but are not limited to:
- Changing examples and case studies so that the broad international range of examples in Teaching and Learning for a Sustainable Future is more regionally or nationally appropriate.
- Changing the examples of education policies provided in some modules to support local or national policy initiatives.
- Keeping the existing case studies and policy examples in order to maintain the global focus of the programme but supplementing them with national examples to increase the local relevance of the programme.

- Changing the learning journal questions eg. by deleting some, adding others, etc.
- Adding sample answers to additional learning journal questions.
- Changing/adding Internet links and data to keep the programme current in terms of statistics and trends in sustainable development and/or education policy.
- Deleting an entire activity from a module or adding an additional one.

Guidelines are provided in the programme to facilitate translation into different languages, along with such adaptations to national and regional contexts.

At the present time, a South African adaptation of the programme is being prepared and plans in hand for its translation into Spanish, Russian and Arabic. UNESCO is keen to establish partnerships that will lead to other adaptations and translations that will lead to the wide adoption of *Teaching and Learning for a Sustainable Future*. This can prove most cost-effective as UNESCO has absorbed all the costs for consultation, development, evaluation and revision and is able to provide the source files and style sheets free of cost for partners.

Conclusion

Teaching and Learning for a Sustainable Future is rooted in a new vision of education, a vision that helps students better understand the world in which they live, addressing the complexity and interconnectedness of problems such as poverty, wasteful consumption, environmental degradation, urban decay, population growth, health, conflict and the violation of human rights that threaten our future. This vision of education emphasises a holistic, interdisciplinary approach to developing the knowledge and skills needed for a sustainable future as well as changes in values, behaviour, and lifestyles. *Teaching and Learning for a Sustainable Future* will enable teachers to plan learning experiences that empower their students to develop and evaluate alternative visions of a sustainable future and to work creatively with others to help bring their visions into effect.

There are over 60 million teachers in the world – and each one is a key agent for bringing about the changes in lifestyles and systems we need. For this reason, innovative teacher education is an important part of educating for a sustainable future. The multimedia format of *Teaching and Learning for a Sustainable Future* means that it is highly flexible and easily adapted. UNESCO welcomes new partners who wish to consider the potential of *Teaching and Learning for a Sustainable Future* as the basis for local projects that can provide for the professional development needs of teachers.

References

Ballantyne, R. Aston, P. (1990): The Provision of Environmental Education Teacher Training in South Africa, Final Report. Department of Environmental and Geographical Science. Capetown: University of Cape Town.

Brinkman, F.G./Scott, W.A.H. (1994): Environmental Education into Initial Teacher Education in Europe (EEITE): the state of the art, ATEE Cahiers No. 8, Brussels: Association of Teacher Education in Europe.

Brinkman, F.G./Scott, W.A.H. (1996): Reviewing a European union initiative on environmental education within programmes of pre-service teacher education, Environmental Education Research, 2 (1), Bath: Carfax.

Bullock, K.M./English, T./Oulton, C.R./Scott, W.A.H. (1996): Reflections on an environmental education staff development initiative for teacher educators, in: Champain, P./Inman S. (eds.), Thinking Futures: Making Space for Environmental Education in ITE – A Handbook for Educators, Godalming: WWF.

CSD (1998): Transfer of Environmentally Sound Technology, Capacity-building, Education and Public Awareness, and Science for Sustainable Development, Report on Sixth Session, Commission on Sustainable Development.

Education Network For Environment and Development (n.d.): Environmental Education and Teacher Education – Preparing for Change and Participation? University of Sussex at Brighton Occasional Paper No. 3.

Fien, J./Heck, D./Ferreira, J. (1997): Learning For A Sustainable Environment, Brisbane: Griffith University for UNESCo-ACEID, Bangkok.

Fien, J./Kumar, P./Ravindranath, M. J. (forthcoming): The Action Research Network as a Strategy for Change: The Learning for a Sustainable Environment Project, Journal of Educational Change.

Hart, P. (1990): Rethinking teacher education environmentally, in Monographs in Environmental Education and Environmental Studies, Vol. VI (Troy, Ohio: North American Association for Environmental Education).

Monroe, M. et al (1993): Toolbox Series 1–5, Ann Arbor: NCEET.

National Institute for Educational Research (1993): The Final Report of a Regional Seminar: Environmental Education and Teacher Education in Asia and the Pacific. Tokyo: National Institute for Educational Research.

National Institute for Educational Research (1996): The Final Report of a Regional Seminar: Learning for a Sustainable Environment: Environmental Education in Teacher Education. Tokyo: National Institute for Educational Research.

Schon, D. (1983): The Reflective Practitioner: How Professionals Think in Action, New York: Basic Books.

Simpson, P./Hungerford, H./Volk, T. (1988): Environmental Education: A Process for Pre-service Teacher Training Curriculum Development, UNESCO-UNEP International Environmental Education Programme, Environmental Education Series No. 26, UNESCO Division of Science, Technical and Environmental Education, Paris.

Spork, H. (1992): Environmental education: A mismatch between theory and practice, Australian Journal of Environmental Education, 8, 147–166.

UNCED (1992): Promoting Education and Public Awareness and Training, Agenda 21, United Nations Conference on Environment and Development, Conches, Ch. 36.

UNESCO (1997): Educating for a Sustainable Future: A Transdisciplinary Vision for Concerted Action, Thessaloniki: UNESCO.

UNESCO (1998): Report of Advisory Group on Teacher Education for Sustainability, Thessaloniki: UNESCO.

UNESCO-ACEID and Griffith University (1994): Final Report of the Planning Group Meeting for the UNESCO-ACEID Project, Learning for a Sustainable Environment - Innovations in Teacher Education. Brisbane: Griffith University.

UNESCO and Griffith University (1993): The Final Report of the UNESCO Asia-Pacific Regional Experts' Meeting on Overcoming the Barriers to Environmental Education through Teacher Education. Brisbane: Griffith University.

UNESCO-UNEP (1976): The Belgrade Charter, Connect, I (1), 1–8.

UNESCO-UNEP (1990): Environmentally Educated Teachers: The Priority of Priorities, Connect, Vol. XV, No. 1, 1–3.

van Rensburg and Lotz, 2000.

Wilke, R.J./Peyton, R.B./Hungerford, H.R. (1987): Strategies for the Training of Teachers in Environmental Education, UNESCO-UNEP International Environmental Education Programme, Environmental Education Series No. 25, Paris: UNESCO Division of Science, Technical and Environmental Education.

Williams, R. (1985): Environmental Education and Teacher Education Project, Report to the Educational Advisory Committee of the World Wildlife Fund (UK), University of Sussex.

Williams, R. (1991): Teacher Education Survey: Environmental Education: Interim Report. Education Network for the Environment and Development, Unpublished.

World Commission on Environment and Development (1987): Our Common Future, Oxford: Oxford University Press.

WWF (1999): Education and Conservation: An Evaluation of the Contributions of Education Programmes to Conservation within the WWF Network. Reference Volume to the Final Report, WWF International & WWF-USA, Gland & Washington.

Rietje van Dam-Mieras, Ron Corvers,
Hans-Peter Winkelmann

ICT and Working Together at a Distance: European Virtual Seminar on Enlargement and Sustainable Development

Sustainable Development

Sustainable development is a complex process the target of which is a balanced interaction between economy, ecology and socio-cultural aspects in development processes. It is interconnected with globalisation, poverty alleviation, social justice, democracy, human rights, peace and environmental protection. A more sustainable development is important to all sectors of society.

The growth of the world population and of the economy, the globalisation of agricultural and industrial production and of the service sector, all contribute to the stress on the environment. Problems in the field of sustainable development are complex problems in which norms and values of different stakeholders, scientific knowledge, uncertainty and dealing with risks all play a role. They ask for a multidisciplinary approach in which the different stakeholders (companies, governments, NGO's, citizens) work together.

Sustainable development not only asks for a dialogue between different actors, it also necessitates a dialogue between different disciplines or better, between persons or groups with different disciplinary backgrounds. Natural sciences are used to analyse the boundary conditions and stability of system earth, social sciences focus on the behaviour of individuals and organisations, and technology is needed for the technological part of the problem solving strategy.

Sustainable development also needs an international approach in which ecological, economical and political interdependencies are discussed by actors from different countries. Actors from different countries will have different social and cultural backgrounds.

Such complex interactions must lead to a responsible reaction to a broad range of challenges which are often rather unpredictable and can be influenced to only a limited extent. In the problem solving process scientific analysis, technological design, laws and regulations, and economic instruments all are needed.

The Enlargement of the European Union

The enlargement process of the European Union is a process of mutual adaptation of the present and new member states. During this process the new member states from Central and Eastern European countries have to adapt their national laws and institutions in order to fit into the European framework. This process of adaptations is dominated by the Aquis Communautaire, a document of about 80000 pages to which the new member states commit themselves. Market economy, good governance principles and social institutions play a prominent role in the adaptation process.

With respect to environmental policy the enlargement procedure is a big challenge for all European states. In 1999 the European Consultative Forum on the Environment and Sustainable Development published a report in which they stated that the enlargement procedure must be understood as one element in a wider process of sustainable development and that the protection of environmental quality should be the overall guiding principle in the enlargement process. This requires integration of environmental protection and sustainable development principles in all relevant policy areas as a key goal of the enlargement process.

We must, however, conclude that in the negotiations accompanying the enlargement process sustainable development does not get the priority the European Consultative Forum on the Environment and Sustainable development stated it should have. There may be many reasons for this, but one main reason probably is that the concept of sustainable development is not internalised in all disciplines. We therefore see it as a task for European Universities to improve the effective integration of sustainable development principles in the enlargement process by making them an obligatory, or at least strongly advised, element in all university curricula.

Sustainable Development and Continuous Change

Of course the European enlargement procedure must be seen against the background of an increased globalisation of the economy and rapid developments in the field of Information and Communication Technology (ICT). The latter weakens the relation between activities and geographical locations. Processes in the production and service sectors can increasingly be spread geographically, electronic markets are emerging, the accessibility of information available world wide is increasing, and the hierarchical structure of organisations is changing.

National governments can manage these developments to only a limited extent because international organisations like OESO, UN, EU, multinationals and NGO's are not limited by borders. In spite of that, national governments should be able to face a broad spectrum of rapidly occurring and rather unpredictable changes in a proactive way. As a consequence there is an increasing need for learning environments that can accommodate both the needs of initial learners and of life long learners.

In Agenda 2000, aimed at a restructuring of the EU finances, structure and policy in perspective of the enlargement of the EU it is suggested that 'knowledge policy' should become one of the key components of European policy. All European citizens should have access to all sources of education. Furthermore it is stated that innovation of these sources is important and therefore 'good practices' in education should be shared as effectively as possible. The Bologna declaration, signed in 1999 by 27 European ministers of education, can be seen as a step forward towards an open European higher education area. We think it is a task of European higher education institutions to give sustainable development a clearly visible position in this European arena.

Sustainable Development and Higher Education

The role of higher education could be seen as preparing citizens for their different roles in society and supporting them life long. This task is more comprehensive than a responsibility for the initial learning trajectories that prepare learners for the labour market, it also comprises life long learning. If this strategy would be adopted, the target group for higher education institutions becomes more heterogeneous.

An additional point to consider is that according to the literature a gradual shift can be seen from a behaviouristic approach of learning to social constructivism. In parallel, a shift from a teacher oriented to a learner oriented approach is found. Learners should not only learn scientific facts, they should also be given the possibility to develop different competencies (cognitive, meta-cognitive, social, affective), and they must be trained in learning and working in multidisciplinary teams.

It is generally agreed that for an optimal learning process the learning environment should be meaningful for each student, irrespective of the faculty or vocational background he or she is coming from. Therefore higher education institutes could specialise in the translation of knowledge from different sources to specific target groups and user contexts. With respect to learning about sustainable development this implies that also the international dimension must be given a place in the learning environment. The application of new ICT tools in the context of learning and teaching deserves serious consideration in this respect, as do organisational matters.

The European Virtual Seminar on Enlargement and Sustainable Development

The seminar focuses on sustainable development in the context of the European enlargement process via a case study approach. After a general introduction on the European Union, its institutions and the enlargement process case studies in the fields of agriculture, energy technology, water management, spatial planning and co-operation in the Euregion Neisse are dealt with.

The didactic concept behind the virtual seminar is that of learning in collaborative learning communities. Because of the use of ICT instruments the members of such communities can be geographically spread over Europe. Student groups in the virtual seminar are not only international, they are also multidisciplinary. The communication within and between the student groups about European enlargement and sustainable development allows for an exchange of ideas and opinions from different parts of Europe.

The institutions that participate in the the European Virtual Seminar are
- the Open University of the Netherlands
- the University of Amsterdam
- the Vrije Universiteit at Amsterdam
- the University of Antwerp
- the University of Extremadura
- Karkonoshe College
- Wroclaw University of Technolgy

- Wroclaw University of Economics, Jelenia Gora Faculty
- Wroclaw University of Agriculture
- the Technical University of Liberec
- the International Graduate School Zittau
- the Hochschule Zittau-Görlitz

The development process is co-ordinated by the Open University of the Netherlands, supported by the COPERNICUS secretariat. The participating institutions co-operatively develop the learning materials en publish web based study materials on the internet. The communication between the students from the different institutions is facilitated by a computer conferencing system.

The time frame for the development of the European Virtual Seminar on Enlargement and Sustainable Development is as follows. In the period october-december 2001 a first experimental seminar is organised with students from some, but not all of the institutions mentioned above. In the period 2002–2003 the experiences are evaluated, the design is improved, and participation of other institutions, especially those in Central and Eastern Europe is organized. Via continuous monitoring and feedback a model for ICT-supported international virtual collaborative learning in the field of sustainability is developed.

We hope that, after this development process, the virtual seminar will turn out to be a valuable instrument for the sharing of knowledge and expertise about sustainable development in the open European higher education area.

Marie-Claude Roland, Anne-Marie Chevre, Joël Chadœuf, Bernard Hubert, Joseph Bonnemaire

Think Forward, Act Now : Training Young Researchers for Sustainability Reshaping the Relationship between PhD Student and Adviser

Introduction

In Europe (Commission SFP 1999)[2], in the United States (Golde/Dore 2001) doctoral studies are being questioned and dissatisfaction is being expressed by both students and faculty, who criticize the relevancy and the efficiency of the training and call for a rethinking of graduate degrees that pays attention to the world. It is commonly argued that the role of science in society must be better taken into account and that a new mode of production of knowledge incorporating the needs and viewpoints expressed by the different stakeholders is emerging which calls into question the adequacy of familiar knowledge producing institutions, whether universities, government research establishments or corporate laboratories (Gibbons et al. 1996). Universities are urged to identify and sponsor new opportunities by which graduate students can employ their learning and abilities to benefit segments of the society beyond the academy. Reasons for dissatisfaction are also found in the attitude of research supervisors : the academic profession is blamed for not meeting professional responsibility in upholding the norms and traditions of their profession through a responsible and ethical conduct (Golde/Dore 2001). And researchers in general are encouraged to seek a "re-shaping of their mutual relationships". Lastly, the fact that, currently, PhD theses tend to be oriented more toward

---

2 See also: The BBSRC Training and Accreditation Programme for Postgraduate Supervisors (TAPPS), http://www.iah.bbsrc.ac.uk/supervisor-training/topics.html.

the production of tools than the exploration of concepts generates more doubts about the possibility to qualify researchers' training as scientific.

Regarding the production of scientific knowledge, the need for crossdisciplinary cooperation is widely acknowledged and emphasized, and scientists agree that historically drawn boundaries of disciplines have to be re-examined and that strategies which lead to fragmentation of knowledge building have to be replaced by practices of integration (Becker/Jahn/Stiess/Wehling n.d.). To overcome the limitations imposed by the fragmentation and segmentation of social scientific knowledge, new competencies are needed, particularly the ability to debate about one's work, to situate it in a collective, collaborative or concerted approach and to build on complementary experiences, competencies, methodologies and viewpoints. Some authors even call for a "re-engineering of our scientific thinking (…) to overcome the limitations that have become evident during the disciplinary and interdisciplinary stages" (Mebratu 2001).

Pressure to change is also exerted through the 5th and 6th European Framework Programmes: building and structuring the European Research Area imply reconsidering, rethinking the role and nature of training through research or for research. Quality and traceability, mobility are matters of extreme importance, the training of young researchers being a key element in the evaluation of both integrated projects and excellence networks. Researchers must assume responsibility for the changes in practices inevitable if they want to achieve these objectives.

In this context, incorporating sustainability into higher education for us means training young researchers who will be able to break new ground in Europe on transdisciplinary issues. It means introducing changes not so much in the teaching (curricula) than in the learning processes. Considering that more than tools, learning abilities and capacity building are sustainable, the issues which must be addressed concern the definition of what can be termed "sustainable training for young researchers" and more generally the representation we share of what being a researcher will mean in the coming years ; they concern the core skills that need to be developed and the criteria to be proposed to assess the sustainability of such training, namely in terms of quality and relevancy. We believe these questions must be addressed and dealt with at the European level, through a joint effort from various places of knowledge such as universities, research institutions, corporate laboratories (Sörlin 2002).

To contribute to the debate and also to the much needed "re-shaping of the relation" between supervisor and student researcher, we present here a training programme developed at INRA, the French National Institute for Agricultural Research. It is based on a cooperating approach between research student and thesis supervisor, who are encouraged to work specifically on the process during which the idea that is born in the supervisor's head is transformed into the student's personal scientific project; epistemology, heuristics and linguistics are among the tools used to generate situations of exploration, dialogue and debate, where participants confront their visions, prejudices or pre-judgments, discover their standpoint and mutually push their "horizons of understanding" (Gadamer 1979). The debates are facilitated by specially trained researchers from 8 different scientific departments of INRA, who form an active network engaged in group learning and reflexivity. Finally training also focuses on the communication competencies expected from researchers.

INRA, a Multidisciplinary Institution Naturally Attentive to the Nature and Quality of Ph.Ds

Let's briefly outline some of INRA's assets in developing and testing a programme that could contribute to a collective reflection on sustainability in graduate and post-graduate education. INRA is a place where agriculture, health and diet, and environment domains converge: it comprises several disciplinary fields (among which agronomy, animal science, animal and plant genetics, microbiology, physiology, economics and sociology), so that the PhDs which are prepared in its laboratories naturally tend to be multidisciplinary. Besides, historically, INRA has forged close links with society, so that again, many PhDs are directly connected to the social demand. Lastly, the Institute with its 8 500 employees, trains about 1 000 PhDs over three years and contributes to thousands of teaching hours.

Reshaping the Relation between Supervisor and Student Researcher using Epistemology, Scientific Debate, Group Learning

We first decided to explore the relation between supervisor and student researcher during the phase of elaboration of the student's research project (first year) to contribute to solving well identified communication difficulties (Roland 1995). In the process, we realized that this collaborative relation could be seen as a model for larger scale situations in the laboratory and became convinced that working with both parties together was essential.

Too little time and space is devoted to exploring the scientific and societal issues at stake in the young researcher's project.

The student researcher's training suffers from the fact that for the past years, research has been turned more toward the "*how's*" than to the "*why's*" of scientific activity : briefly, little space and time is devoted to exploring the long- and medium-term scientific and societal objectives of a research project while attention focuses on the methods and tools to be used, tested or designed. Our research on scientific writing practices (Roland 1995) confirms that, despite existing writing standards[3] and editors' and referees' comments and

---

3   American National Standard Institute, Standard for the writing of scientific papers (ANSI Z39.16–1979) and of scientific abstracts (ANSI Z39.14–1979). French National Standard Institute (Association Française de Normalisation, AFNOR) Standard for the writing of scientific papers and scientific abstracts (AFNOR, NF Z 44-004).

recommendations, a large majority of scientific papers, and more generally a large amount of the scientific written production, concentrates on what was done and observed and not on the issues at stake or the questions addressed.

No wonder therefore that the student researcher is often considered as a highly qualified technician and does not always share the objectives of his supervisor and of the research team he belongs to, let alone the objectives and scope of the larger project (European, regional or other) which finances his own project. Moreover the oral or written exercises he is frequently asked to do inside the laboratory consist in presenting the results of his work, which very seldom leads to debating the "*what's*" and "*why's*" of the research and the relevancy of some choices. Oral presentations like written reports will most of the time focus on tasks, experiments, methods and tools.

We need to create "ideal speech situations"

Habermas (1984) defines what he calls an "ideal speech situation" as a situation where each participant has an effective equality of chances to take part in dialogue; where asymmetry is limited, where dialogue is unconstrained and not distorted. What the idea of an ideal speech situation does is to provide us with some ways of identifying and exploring the distortions that exist.

In the scientific community, communication is hindered by the extreme specialization of research activities, and particularly by the fact that researchers "learn their trade" in the laboratory and that much of the knowledge and know how, which are transmitted and acquired through a process of socialization, will remain tacit and implicit. Communication therefore must be fostered. Concepts and terminology in particular must be debated and clarified, researchers must be encouraged to produce informative rather than descriptive statements : going through these mental, intellectual activities, researchers question their own discourse, its relevancy, the relevancy of the knowledge and know how they are transmitting and eventually they will improve and enhance their relevancy. The process is certainly difficult and costly in terms of self image and authority but researchers will gain in objectivity and capacity to convince.

At INRA, because of the multidisciplinary research environment, PhD research projects tend to be situated at the frontiers of disciplines and research fields. So we create such speech and communication situations by inviting several research department members, who are keen to build a shared vision and want to identify new questions, to participate to seminars: *Réflexives* are usually organized with three or four scientific departments, outside the laboratory, which means that participants (supervisors and their PhD students) are allowed to work together outside hierarchy. This condition is essential to the process. The seminars are organized in workshops with 4 to 5 supervisor/student pairs, the debate being mediated by facilitators: the facilitators are researchers from several departments of the Institute who believe in fostering dialogue between disciplines and re-structuring the training process of student researchers. They have received a special training: first they have taken part in *Réflexives* sessions as participants and experienced debating their own work; then they have acquired facilitation techniques . They are organized in an active network which regularly meets to share experience, discuss facilitation strategies and methods as well as analyse the impact of *Réflexives* on student researchers' training. Their role is to encourage fundamental communication activities like listening – paying attention to what is said and how it is said –, questioning, re-formulating to limit the use of jargon and specific codes, to make one's ideas explicit. Their role as facilitators is reinforced by the fact that they belong to other disciplinary fields, thus bringing with the other participants multi-disciplinary point of views in the debate. To facilitate the whole process, they use several techniques, among which that of mind-mapping (Buzan 1995) specially adapted for a public of researchers. *Réflexives* focus also on the other major activity which requires creativity, rigor and relevance, that is communication in writing: workshops are organized where participants' written productions (abstracts, scientific papers or reports) are criticized using linguistics tools and methods, under the guidance of a linguist. The participants, analyse their texts through a process which includes reading, questioning the concepts or the value of statements and examining language. This analysis process generates scientific debate of course, and discussion of scientific practices – writing practices, mimetic conduct, training practices, etc.

Providing a Model for Formulating Research Questions or Research Problems by Working with the Pair Supervisor/Ph.D Student

Working with the pair supervisor/student researcher on the elaboration and communication phases of the student's research project is certainly the major innovation brought by *Réflexives*. We shall consider here first what both parties – supervisor and student - gain from working together through a structured process including reflexivity and group learning, how innovative the activities proposed in *Réflexives* are, before discussing their sustainability.

The Ph.D student's research activity, method and objectives are clarified by having him explain his work in simple words to people from various disciplines.

Jargon obstructs clarity and threatens quality. It also contributes to those distortions which hamper dialogue (Habermas 1984). Surrounded by colleagues from various disciplines or lay persons, the student researcher is forced to formulate what remains tacit in the laboratory: his research problem, research question, research strategy, etc. This process is very often a difficult one because it requires reflection on one's own work and choices and requires also to assume a well defined point of view (Prieto 1975; Darré 1999); that's when the student comes very close to "experiencing" epistemology . The presence of colleagues from other disciplines and of facilitators guarantee also to both student and advisor an effective equality of chances in dialogue . Freed from most hierarchical ties and competition, the debate is very open : new approaches are suggested or explored, concepts are confronted, arguments developed, logical sequences and relations enhanced, terminology discussed. The student realizes that knowledge is not a fixed thing or commodity to be grasped. It is not something "out there" waiting to be discovered. Rather, it's an aspect of a process (Gadamer 1979; LEARN Group 2000). *Réflexives* contribute to broaden participants' scientific culture and leads the Ph.D student to position his work in a broader context than usual.

Although the objective of the exercise is not to influence the participants into modifying their point of view and their objectives, it often happens that the research question is not only clarified but modified.

The supervisor becomes learner.

The presence of the supervisor is crucial. In the interaction with his student, he will realize how much the apprentice researcher knows, has understood of what he has tried to convey ; he will also realize if key information is missing, has never been given or has been taken for granted, and realize also that misunderstandings are plenty. He will identify and explore the distortions that exist and be better prepared to remedy them.

Beyond this analysis, he will reflect on the relevancy of the question proposed, of the adequacy of the methods and tools chosen and *in fine* he will reflect on his own scientific project, assess its relevancy and probably think of elements he had consciously or unconsciously set aside or ignored, imagine new paths to be explored and new collaborations to build. Like their students, supervisors experience epistemology and reflexivity.

The Ph.D student is at the center of the debate.

Physically speaking first, the student researcher is the one being questioned, interest focuses on him, and at the center of the mind-map is his research question or scientific objective. Then *Réflexives* provide him with the opportunity to formulate his own, personal vision of his project using his own words. Working with supervisor/student researcher pairs, we very often realize how mimetic, even symbiotic the relation can be. The words are the same, the sentences are duplicates one of the other, there is no real dialogue. Similarly, evaluators will confess that it is very often difficult to identify a candidate's contribution (PhD student at a thesis presentation or researcher in scientific papers or project). Therefore it is crucial to allow the student researcher to use his own terms, build his own discourse about the research he is doing. As noted by T. Gaudin (1998), the supervisor's mission is to accompany the student researcher through a crucial process of changing status, i.e the latter must "turn away from a passive role, which has consisted in absorbing established knowledge to a pro-active role which consists in transforming knowledge into creations."

Lastly, placed in a central position, the student reflects about his own choices during the research and beyond ; he tries to explore relations : how does his present research activity in a particular field relate to his own personal project? Can he figure out the competencies he will acquire? Has he gained autonomy? How does he relate to the research team? He is challenged to think beyond his everyday activity, and to reflect about his motivations for action, the meanings and value of his research and of course to consider the limits of fragmented knowledge.

The sustainability of the training is guaranteed through situations of reflexivity and group learning, and reinforced by the institution.

As indicated before, the structured process at work in the seminars presupposes that advisers are considered not as teachers but as learners, but that in all cases they identify themselves as group members.

Thus conditions are favourable for all participants to think critically about the re-structuring of the training process, and to decide to embark on new ways of working together: they have been given the opportunity to re-learn their way to interact, to re-think and re-shape their mutual relationships.

Let's now consider how sustainable the innovative activities of *Réflexives* are, and how the sustainability of the training is reinforced by the Institution itself. As Holen & al. remind us, "the material conditions and staff engagement prevailing at the institute are crucial factors for the practical implementation of alternative ways of teaching and the integration of interdisciplinary forms of teaching in courses" (Van den Bor/Holen/Wals/Leal Filho n.d.). The US report "At Cross Purposes" came to the same conclusion: "No real gains can be accomplished unless the performance of instructors, both graduate teaching assistants and faculty is exceptional and focused squarely on the needs of students to acquire an education that will prepare them for the 21st century" (Golde/Dore 2001). *Réflexives* started as a means to meet the communication needs identified by a scientific director within his research department. But it very quickly drew the attention and participation of a growing number of scientific departments within INRA : three years later, in 1999, 15 out of the 17 departments had participated at least once to the workshops proposed. Throughout the process, we were careful to make heads of departments "co-owners of the innovation". As for the administrative body, they obviously support this collaborative approach : first considered as a pilot pedagogical experiment by the institution, the project has taken a new dimension when the Board of Directors recently decided that it was crucial for the much needed renewal of competencies in the Institute. Yet among the 15 departments who acknowledge the need for such places of debate and exchange and sponsor *Réflexives*, only three so far have developed an internal organization to provide support for their student researchers and accompany the work of supervisors. More implication could be expected that would allow for experience sharing, for the development of tools and methods and would reinforce the existing dynamics; hopefully, we can see things evolving : researchers in charge of policy-making and of the training of young researchers are more and more involved and keen to promote changes.

Conclusions and Perspectives

Réflexives already contribute to identify and enrich transdisciplinary issues as well as to build collectively the new competencies the institution needs to tackle those issues. Other collective arenas of debate and interactions must be imagined and opened, to develop new modes of scientific communication. We believe the pedagogical set up, functioning and methods of *Réflexives* can be used to work on larger scientific projects : we have already worked with scientists from many disciplines and from government and corporate laboratories to design and build the projects of teams within the Institute and to build large European projects, and more generally to develop understanding between communities and elaborate new scientific questions or objectives.

But among the questions which must be addressed now because of the changes brought in terms of professional development, that of the criteria is crucial: first to give student researchers means to assess their training because, as noted in the report "At Cross purposes" (Golde/ Dore 2001) "many students do not understand the criteria used to determine when they will be ready to graduate. Most disciplines indicated 40-50 percent of respondents being clear on this point, but lab sciences scored the lowest, with molecular biology and chemistry both less than 25 percent". Second, to define and evaluate the sustainability of young researchers' training: so far the surveys and proposals for a re-thinking of the missions of supervisors have been based on the criteria presently available (scientific excellence, relevance and quality of the research methods, project construction, etc.): but are such criteria sustainable? Do they need to be reconsidered and new ones formulated? Collaborative work at the European level is necessary if we want to enhance quality, traceability of research activities and mobility within the European Research Area; it is also necessary if we want to bring places of knowledge production or creation closer to the surrounding society in order to contribute, in D. Mebratu's words (Mebratu 2001), to "achieving civic competency". Innovation in students' training will benefit all spheres of society.

References

Becker E./Jahn, Th./Stiess, I./Wehling P. (n.d.): Sustainability: A cross disciplinary concept for social transformations, Management of Social Transformations, MOST Policy Papers 6, Unesco.

Buzan, T. (1995): The MindMap Book, BBC Books.

Commission SFP (1999): Gaining professional experience in research. Reshaping doctoral training, French Physics Society, a report prepared by the "Commission SFP pour la réforme des formations doctorales", Jan.1999. http://sfp.in2p3.fr/.

Darré, J.P. (1999): La production de connaissances pour l'action, Ed. Maison des Sciences de l'homme, INRA, Paris.

Gadamer, H.G. (1979): Truth and Method, London, Sheed and Ward.

Gaudin, T. (1998): De l'innovation, Ed. De l'Aube.

Gibbons M. et al. (1996): The New Production of Knowledge, SAGE Publications.

Golde, C. M./Dore, T. M. (2001): At Cross Purposes: what the experiences of doctoral students reveal about doctoral education. A report prepared for The Pew Charitable Trusts, Philadelphia, PA. http://www.phd-survey.org.

Habermas, J. (1984): The Theory of Communicative Action, Cambridge, Polity Press.

LEARN Group (2000): Cow up a tree: Knowing and learning for change in agriculture; case studies from industrial countries, INRA.

Mebratu, D. (2001): The Knowledge Dimension of the Sustainability Challenge, International Journal of Economic Development, 3(1).

Prieto, L. (1975): Pertinence et pratique, Paris, Ed. de Minuit.

Roland, M.C. (1995): Analyse des Pratiques Scripturales des Chercheurs, Thèse de l'Université de Grenoble III- Stendhal, Didactique et Sciences du Langage.

Sörlin, S. (2002): Cultivating the Places of Knowledge, Swedish Institute for Studies of Education and Research (SISTER), Working paper 2002-9.

Van den Bor, W./Holen, P./Wals, A./Leal Filho, W. (n.d.): Integrating Concepts of Sustainability into Education for Agriculture and Rural Development, Peter Lang AG.

Wilfried P.M.F. Ivens

New Ways of Academic Education: Chances for Sustainability

Introduction

Society is facing rapid changes: individualisation, internationalisation and digitalisation are detectable in all sectors of society. In this short contribution a quick scan is given of the major consequences of these changes for education in general and education in sustainable development in particular. What opportunities for education in sustainability arise from these changes? How can these opportunities be realised?

Trends in education

In education a slow but steady trend towards increasingly individualised leaning paths is emerging. In this process, three sub-processes can be distinguished. Firstly, there is a tendency to pay more attention to *competence learning*. Thus teaching is more focused on the enhancement of the ability of individual students to integrate knowledge, attitudes and skills in the right way at the right moment. Secondly, the importance of *dual mode education*, i.e. the combination of working and learning, is growing. Thirdly, it is generally accepted that learning does not stop once a university degree has been obtained. *Life-long learning* is becoming more and more crucial in anyone's career. All these three sub-processes originate from the needs of individual students in their specific situation.

With regard to *internationalisation* the educational field, especially in Europe, is rapidly evolving. International exchange of students is regarded as an indispensable component of modern curricula. Educational institutes are co-operating more and more beyond national borders. Internationalisation is stimulated by ongoing developments in *information and communication technology*. Furthermore, these new technologies give new opportunities to design student centred open learning environments.

Characteristics of Education in Sustainable Development

What are the key elements of education on sustainability issues? Scholars agree that an *interdisciplinary approach* is indispensable when studying sustainability matters. Knowledge of the concepts of other disciplines and the ability to co-operate in multidisciplinary teams is a *sine qua non* for future 'sustainability-experts'. Moreover, the sustainability issue is to be dealt with in a *societal context*. To be able to face complex and persistent sustainability issues students must be trained in the usage of techniques stimulating *creativity*. Clearly, an international orientation for students in sustainability is of major importance; the problems we are facing are transnational or even global; legislation is increasingly laid down by international bodies; companies are operating internationally more and more.

Need of New Structure

Does the present education meet the demands with respect to the general trends in education and the specific characteristics of education in sustainability issues described above? A quick scan of European curricula reveals that in general curricula are short of: 1) relevant practical skills, 2) experiences with teamwork, 3) individualised learning paths, 4) active learner participation, 5) interaction between theory and practice, 6) interdisciplinarity, 7) international exchange, 8) project organisation, 9) creativity development.

In a widespread number of educational institutes individual elements of the above summation have been incorporated in curricula. However, there is still a long way to go before all these aspects have been integrated into a consistent educational model. To accelerate these innovative developments, experiences should be brought together.
Education on sustainable development would benefit from a new network structure that accommodates: 1) an efficient sharing of good practices, knowledge, materials, methods, and experiences, 2) an efficient international collaboration of both teachers and students and 3) a connection of academia and society (public - private partnerships). Such a structure should provide an international network where students and tutors can meet to exchange ideas. The network structure should, furthermore, stimulate collaboration between students and provide possibilities for students to study specific topics on sustainability.

A Virtual Sustainability Agency

A structure as proposed above could be shaped as a Virtual Sustainability Agency (see figure 1). The core of such a network structure consists of three elements: 1) a co-ordination centre, 2) student teams (international and interdisciplinary) and 3) a knowledge base (clearing house).

Tutors of the participating academic institutions staff the co-ordination centre. This centre for example deals with student intakes, provides advices on individual competence learning and student assessments.

The knowledge base consists of methods and materials that can be of use for the student teams to carry out project work, e.g. tools for sustainable design or creativity workshops. Initially, materials for the clearinghouse are provided by the participating institutes based on existing 'old' materials.

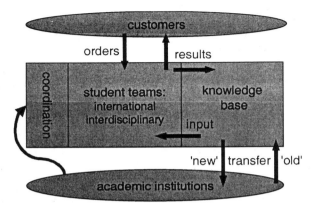

Figure 1 Schematic representation of a Virtual Sustainability Agency

The external 'real' world plays an important role in this network structure. Orders for the agency are obtained from *customers*: private companies and governmental and non-governmental organisations. The student teams carry out these orders. Project results are reported to the clients, while derivates from this, like scenario studies, model calculations or results from literature searches, can be entered into the knowledge base. Finally, the results can be transferred to the participating academic institutes for usage in their educational programmes.

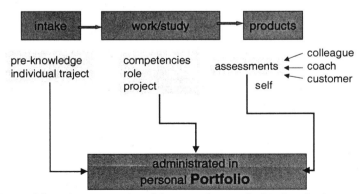

Figure 2 Schematic representation of the personal approach of students in the agency

During their work for the agency the participating students should be focussed on their individual learning objectives. Preferably personal competence development and project tasks should be based on an individual intake. While working for the agency the students should reflect on their work and behaviour. Systematic assessment by peers could be a useful tool for this (see figure 2).

This entire structure should, preferably, be realised in an electronic working and learning environment. Such a virtual environment enables participation independent of place and time.

Utopian or Realistic?

A network structure providing study, work and exchange of new materials and ideas in an integrated way within a virtual environment is not a utopian construct. Actually such networks exist already, however until now in general on a small scale. One example is the Virtual Environmental Consultancy Agency (VECA) which is run by the Open University of the Netherlands in close co-operation with other Dutch educational institutes. An extended description of the concept behind the VECA is given elsewhere: Westera & Sloep, 1998 and Westera et al (2000). A short description of the VECA, based on these publications, is given below.

The Virtual Environmental Consultancy Agency (VECA) attempts to fully integrate learning and working in a distance education environment. This is unlike case-based and problem-based approaches, where, generally, the 'working' aspect is lacking. In the VECA we try to generate a networked learning environment resembling an authentic professional situation. Students working in the VECA address real orders on behalf of real external customers, and deliver real products. Therefore the VECA is *not* an extended role-playing game, which usually represent self-contained business simulations.

The VECA is not restricted to a fixed location on the premises of the educational institute, but is located in cyberspace, i.e. mediated via a computer network. It thus combines the flexibility that is so characteristic of distance learning — students are at liberty to choose time, pace and place — with the desired integration of learning and working. The VECA thus narrows the gap between theory and practice. Another rather unique feature is that the VECA is able to address individual needs, because it works with individualised learning contracts. Along the same lines, it fosters a relationship between tutors and students that differs significantly from the patterns common in education: not the educators are in control of the VECA, the students run the business. In the VECA students are stimulated to rely on themselves, to act autonomously and responsibly in their confrontation with the complexities of the real world. The educators mainly monitor and watch over the efficacy and quality of learning. Finally, like case-based and problem-based approaches the VECA supports active learner participation, takes on problem solving in complex environments, and promotes teamwork.

Within the VECA, all processes are dominated by the concept of *competence learning*: learn how to complete tasks by integrating complexes of knowledge, skills and attitudes. *Competence counsellors*, who are members of the educational staff, assess new students. In this intake procedure students reveal their learning needs, and the competency counsellors include these into the competence map so as to arrive at student specific competence gaps. Collectively, the competence gaps constitute the student's *career plan* in the company. The career plan is subsequently used as the starting point for assigning sensible tasks to the students.

Tasks are derived from the *orders* obtained from external customers. Once accepted, an order is decomposed into a number of distinct *tasks* that can be distributed over individual students. As any order consists of numerous tasks, students work in project teams, headed by a *project manager* (also a student) who is responsible for the delivery of an advice that is both on time and up to the marks. Other specific functions for students are e.g. *knowledge manager*, *consultant* (on a specific domain) or member of the *communication staff*.

Note that this task assignment strategy primarily aims to fill the competence gaps of student-workers. It is thus quite hazardous in terms of overall business success. While it prevents the employees from performing routine jobs, it principally advocates the idea of incompetence at work. This is the price to be paid if learning comes first and running a business only second. So from an educational point of view this is quite a healthy situation.

An extensive system is established which monitors and assesses student's (in)competencies. It includes traditional *teacher controlled evaluation* (co-assessment) procedures as well as methods for *self- and peer-assessment* by the students themselves. The latter are used to assess the individual's informal knowledge and functioning.

All documents produced in the course of a student's career – i.e. results of assessments along with reports and papers produced on behalf of customers, etc. – are collected in a personal *portfolio* that forms the basis of establishing and formalising performance levels. By asking the customers to assess the final report's merit in relation to the order originally submitted by them, an external assessment of the student's work is made. This too is incorporated in the portfolio. Collectively these assessments also reflect on the effectiveness and the quality of the teaching of the entire learning environment. Based on the portfolio the examiner establishes a final mark for each individual student (figure 3).

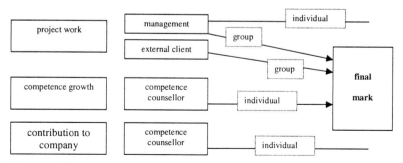

Figure 3   Schematic presentation of the final assessment in the VECA

Concluding

International educational panels are on the move. A heavily loaded "innovation train" thunders through the educational landscape. For educators with commitment towards education on sustainability issues it is important to hop on this train. Time is ripe for further initiatives towards international networks for virtual learning and working on sustainability issues. With the help of new information and communication technologies students and tutors from nations far apart can efficiently study and work together and exchange their ideas, methods and materials.

References

Westera, W./Sloep, P.B. (1998): The Virtual Company: towards a self-directed, competence-based learning environment. Educational Technology, Vol. 38 (1), pp. 32–38.

Westera, W./Sloep, P.B./Gerrissen, J.F. (2000): The design of the Virtual Company: synergism of learning and working in a networked environment. Innovations in Education and Training International 37 (1), pp. 24–33.

III.
Translating Theory into Practice

Gerd Michelsen

Higher Education and Sustainable Development in Germany: The Example of the University of Lüneburg

Introduction

This article should give in the first place an overview on the developments in higher education for sustainable development in Germany. In the second place, the example of the University of Lüneburg is described to illustrate the recent developments and future prospects on the basis of a case study.

In 2001, two extensive reports concerning the state and perspectives of education for sustainable development in Germany have been published. One report which has been requested by the German Bundestag. The second one was published by the German Länder (or State) Presidents. While the federal government put emphasis on federal activities – based on their limited jurisdiction in education topics – the German Länder Presidents reported about the activities in the Länder.

These reports were preceded by two big congresses in the last two years. They both tried to discuss previous developments and further consequences for education for sustainable development from the "development" and "environment" perspectives. In September 2000, the Development Policy Association of German Non-Governmental Organizations (VENRO) hosted the congress "Education 21 – Learning for fair and sustainable development" with 700 participants in Bonn in September 2000. The 2001 congress, "Learning and designing future" with 500 participants from all education fields, had been prepared by different groups of experts. 70 best-practice examples were presented. Besides school-, work-, university- and extracurricular education, issues of co-operation with industry and the local authorities as well as the opportunities for new media were discussed.

Education for Sustainable Development in Germany – a Brief Overview

A significant rapid development has taken place in Germany over the last years: from an environmental education oriented towards environmental protection, we are now moving towards a multi-dimensional education for sustainable development. Education for sustainable development has entered into different fields of educational practice. It is also found in both formal and informal educational processes.

Often, most of the different initiatives, activities and offers assign themselves to the traditional fields of nature protection and environmental education, but sometimes also to education for sustainable development. Additionally, a lot of different best-practice examples exist that show which structural basic conditions, which foundations as regards content and which new teaching and learning cultures are needed for a wider implementation of education for sustainable development.

Within the frame of a common education planning, the work of the Bund-Länder Commission for Educational Planning and Research Promotion (BLK) has to be highlighted. An important resolution by the BLK in this sense is the orientation framework "Education for Sustainable Development" from 1998. It formulates didactical principles and key qualifications for an education for sustainable development. Furthermore, the tasks in different educational fields to further implement the framework of sustainable development are described in detail. The orientation framework suggests concrete federal and Länder actions that include the innovative, organisational and transferring levels.

Within the frame of common education planning by the federal government and Länder, the BLK-programme "21" is currently carried out. The federal education ministry (BMBF) supports the programme with 15 Länder over the period of five years. Its goal is to integrate education for sustainable development into school practice. The programme shall help to further spread the innovative first steps towards education for sustainable development by the individual schools that are involved in the programme. A dissemination of the tested programme modules will be started as early as possible. In its concept, the programme "21" refers strongly to the participation idea of Agenda 21.

The BLK has also sponsored the above mentioned congress "Learning and designing future – Education for Sustainable Development" in Osnabrück in June 2001.

During this congress, different deficits within the field of education for sustainable development were identified:
- There is a lack of systematic and empirical knowledge about the state of education for sustainable development. This deficit extends over all educational fields.
- Though some positive first signs can be found, the integration of environmental education and development-related education into an education for sustainable development happens very slowly.
- Education for sustainable development is fixed and spread differently in the individual educational fields. An advanced development level has been achieved in school education – not least thanks to the BLK-programme "21". Other educational fields do not look as good.
- With regard to a concrete implementation of education for sustainable development, the qualification of the different actors in the individual educational fields is still inadequate.
- A debate about questions that are connected theoretically and practically with the education for sustainable development is made more difficult by institutional barriers like dominance of individual sciences, stiff structures, transfer of research results.

- The research of education for sustainable development is insufficient. It lacks concepts for quality management and reception research, following previous work in the field of environmental education.
- The support structures for regional initiatives of co-operating participants are too weak. They hinder social engagement that is very important for the acceptance of sustainable development. This concerns primarily the engagement of teenagers.

Which perspectives follow from that and which conclusions can be drawn?

Perspectives and Consequences

The countries that signed the Agenda 21 in Rio were asked to develop a strategy that aims at an economically competitive, socially fair and ecologically sustainable development. This task has been taken up by Germany as well; a national strategy of sustainability was being developed. Education and research politics serve as a basic for this national strategy of sustainability. Education and research – in the federal government's opinion – are fundamental requirements for a permanent protection of natural living conditions, the preservation of an economic ability of competition and the fair distribution of work, income and life chances.

The federal government and the Länder stand together in front of the dual challenge in German education politics: on one hand, supportive frame conditions for the acquisition of knowledge and competences that are decisive for the future of individuals as well as for our whole society have to be created. On the other hand, it has to be taken care that despite the increasing quality requirements social exclusion can be avoided and reduced.

There are the following possibilities to further develop education for sustainable development for the next years:
- The different centres of competence in our society have to be connected stronger; new incentive structures through the use of new media have to be created. By this, the wide competences and the extensive fact knowledge of research and educational practice shall be made transparent and more easy available for all who are interested in issues of education for sustainable development.
- The national and international dialogue of education for a sustainable development has to be supported further.
- The transfer of research results about topics of sustainability in education has to be intensified. The stronger integration of education and communication aspects in research and education projects serves as a basis. It is the goal to transfer the necessary orientation and acting knowledge for concrete steps relevant to sustainability into educational practice in the required extent. Transfer places between university and research organisations outside the university as well as the educational practice shall contribute considerably to this.
- The co-operation of local participants has to be improved by founding and extension of regional networks or regional learning structures. The participation of a wider population in learning processes about sustainable development has to be supported. Through co-operation with local participants, sustainable structuring measures within the education field can be initiated.
- International co-operations and programmes of education for sustainable development have to be extended and intensified. This shall be done by an intensification of trans-national projects of education for sustainable development within the frame of different programmes on the European Union or similar levels.

The federal and Länder governments estimate that education for sustainable development will be further supported and sponsored in Germany over the next couple of years. The important goal has to be that education for sustainable development will become a natural task in every educational field. It will be decisive how educational institutions, the universities in particular, will react to these challenges.

In summary, one can determine that an extremely large number of projects and measures in all educational areas has been developed. These intentions also include the combination of formal and informal educational processes. In this case it is obvious that, besides formal education institutions, especially Local Agenda 21 initiatives have initiated a number of co-operations for education for sustainable development. Also, non-governmental organisations (NGOs) and institutions with their own "Agenda-profile" (especially "one world-institutions" and environmental centers) are active in this field. Primarily, these activities are related to the opening of schools and informal further education, but also to university initiatives.

The *positive trends* can be summarized as follows:
- Through the implementation of education for sustainable development, a coupling of social engagement and education for sustainable development is being achieved. Additionally, environmental education is being combined with participative learning.
- The implementation for education for sustainable development fosters the co-operation between formerly separately acting fields (environmental education - global learning).
- The implementation for education for sustainable development connects to the further development of educational institutions into a "learning organisation."
- The implementation for education for sustainable development supports the development of school networks and regional co-operation activities.

From this, the necessary *requirements* for political action can be derived:
- Incentives for interdisciplinary co-operation and projects in all educational institutions (e.g. curricula, examination guidelines) and during job training.

- Supporting educational institutions to do programmatic work (e.g. identification of objectives and main thematic emphasis; evaluation; co-operation with external partners).
- Support of regional networks and model regions (coordinating offices, co-operation projects, transfer of experience, evaluation).

The University of Lüneburg as a German Example

As one of the first German universities, the University of Lüneburg in the northern state of Lower Saxony has launched its internal "agenda process" in 1999 to pursue the implementation of sustainable development into university routine. The university's self-governing bodies have made several important decisions to get the process underway. Since 1997, the University of Lüneburg has been undertaken the following steps in order to implement sustainable development:
- participation in the action program by the Conference of Rectors, Presidents and Vice Chancellors of the European Universities (CRE) based on the "Copernicus Charter" for sustainable development,
- decision to establish a commission "University and Agenda 21" and to appoint an agenda representative,
- decision to lay emphasis research on "environmental quality targets and biodiversity" and "Agenda 21",
- decision on "Environmental Principals of the University of Lüneburg" and last, but not least
- decision on "Guidelines for Sustainable Development at the University of Lüneburg" in spring of 2000 (see last chapter in this article).

A further background for the university's agenda process is provided by the statewide agenda process in Lower Saxony where the realization of the agenda 21 process has been started in December of 1996. At the same time, participation was also suggested to the state's universities. The federal state programme "Sustainable Development in

Lower Saxony", which was passed by of the Lower Saxony Government in November 1997, puts a lot of attention to the universities. The programme points out: *"The goal is ... a systematic realization of agenda ideas at the Lower Saxony universities as a central task, that is driven by the care about a common future where everyone takes responsibility"* (Niedersächsisches Umweltministerium 1997, p. 30). The conclusion of the intermediate report of "Roundtables Agenda 21 in Lower Saxony" in December 1997 was similar (Runder Tisch Agenda 21). The goal was confirmed at a joint conference "University and Agenda 21" of the Evangelic Academy of Loccum and the Lower Saxony University Conference. Also, the necessity to make corresponding steps at the universities, which take the implementation of agenda ideas in research, teaching and further education into consideration and which aim at changing processes inside the institution, too, was underlined (Loccum 1997).

Given this background, the development of the project idea "Agenda 21 and the University of Lüneburg" was initiated. This project is quite unusual: on one hand, it is a development project, through which prerequisites for a change towards sustainable work, life and resource management patterns shall be created. On the other hand, it is a research project with the objective to try out and evaluate the requirements and opportunities for innovations at the university in the sense of the concept of sustainable development.

The perspectives of ecological, economic, social and cultural development that have to be integrated in a concept of sustainable development are addressed by the individual elements of the whole project:
- Eco-Audit: Validation of the university according to EMAS.
- University campus as part of daily life: This project deals with the question how communication and consumption patterns can be designed on the university campus in order to contribute to the process towards sustainability.
- Sustainability and Arts: This project focuses on questions of sustainable development using arts as a main theme.

- Teaching, Interdisciplinarity and Sustainable Development: Through the development of an interdisciplinary and interdepartmental study program, all students shall be given the opportunity of additional qualification. Additionally, the introduction of sustainability into teaching shall be discussed.
- Energy Management of the University: The university's energetic situation shall be improved by technical and non-technical means; students shall learn contents and methods of sustainable development in practical, project-orientated teaching.
- Information, Public Outreach and Transfer: Information and discussion rounds shall be offered to university staff and the general public (e.g. through the project's own newspaper) in order to broaden the general understanding of sustainability.

The project's structure already considers certain requirements of a work environment according to sustainable development:
- All part projects are supervised by colleagues from different departments of the university: an interdisciplinary and interdepartmental approach is the baseline.
- Student work groups have been integrated in all part projects; this way, we try to allow participation as demanded in Agenda 21
- University staff from the administration have been included in the projects, especially the ones of energetic optimization, eco-audit validation and university campus as part of our daily lives. Also, further education courses for university staff are offered.
- External institutions have been integrated in the projects. The university also participates in Lower Saxony's Agenda 21-process, co-operates with other universities in both Germany and foreign countries and with local Agenda 21-processes in the Lüneburg region.
- Different kinds of knowledge and experience can be seen in the part projects; among those many resulting from different functions and points of view of different people from the university. Experiences from our daily lives play an important role as much as the standpoint of external co-operating partners. A focus is put on the cul-

ture of the different scientific disciplines. They form the basis for scientific working methods, but even lead to the development of different professional shapings. All these can be interpreted as clusters of life styles which are developed from the discipline's specific self-understanding, the expected professional status and biographical experiences which are all important for the decision in favor of a certain scientific discipline.

Within the framework of the project, making aware of the different kinds of knowledge and experience will contribute to put the requirements for the development of participating, inter- and transdisciplinary working methods within the course of studies, teaching and research all as a contribution to innovative processes of sustainable development at universities in concrete forms.

What has been done so far? Although it is almost impossible to give a complete picture of the whole process, the following interim balance can provide an overview:
- In May 2000, the University of Lüneburg was validated and certified according to EMAS as one of the first European universities. The implementation of an environmental management system is underway. The university's chancellor, who is responsible for this, is supported by and receives advice from an environmental committee which consists of members of all different university faculties. As a first step, a waste separating system for the whole campus has been introduced. Meanwhile, a campaign for optimizing the use of energy has gotten into full swing.
- Since summer 2000, the university offers a new three-semester study program "Sustainability" to all interested students for further qualification in addition to their general course of studies. This interdisciplinary program is orientated towards practical experience. Students receive an university certificate upon successful completion and a presentation of a special project. Additionally, it is currently being discussed if and how aspects of sustainability may be included in all programs offered by the university. After the revision of the

program the university will start with the new program in 2003.
- The social dimension of sustainability is (among other approaches) being addressed through a dialogue about the different understandings of the institution "university" itself that have been developed by the groups represented at the university. Therefore, the center of attention is directed to communication processes that support the interaction between students, teachers and other employees. For this purpose, the so-called "Agenda-Café" has been established. It should also be used as a cultural institution (different events such as lectures, readings and cabaret). In 2001 a new project was started with the focus on the context of sustainability, health and university.
- The "Campus Courier" newsletter has been established to further discuss ideas and thoughts about sustainability inside and outside the university campus. It is published once a semester and reports not only about university projects, but also other initiatives and activities on sustainability. The newsletter is free. In addition to that, a publication series "University Innovations – Sustainable Development" has been initiated to emphasize the scientific discussion of "sustainable universities".
- Furthermore, the idea of an internal agenda process at a university is being tested and discussed at conferences and workshops. Worth mentioning are the "Sustainable University" conference of January 2000 and the workshop "Ethics and Sustainability" held in November 2000, where the role of different sciences within the sustainability discourse were discussed. Another major event was the organization of the International COPERNICUS-Conference on "Higher Education for Sustainability: Towards the World Summit for Sustainable Development", which was held 8-10 October 2001. The major outcome of this conference was the "Lüneburg Declaration on Higher Education for Sustainable Development" that addressed the Johannesburg-Summit. This conference constituted the first COPERNICUS conference in Germany and underscored the important role the University of Lüneburg is playing in the COPERNICUS network. Also, the agenda process is accompa-

nied by different arts events featuring internationally known artists.

So far, the University of Lüneburg's agenda process has provided a lot of new impulses so far. Certainly, they will lead to permanent changes at the university: changes in the daily routine, in teaching, in interaction between the university and its surroundings or in the personal life of every single university member.

Guidelines of the University of Lüneburg for Sustainability

A. Preamble

In view of the threats to the natural resources and the increasing inequities among people and societies and in the light of the responsibility to enable future generations a self-determined life, the University of Lüneburg expresses its self-commitment for a sustainable development according to Article 20 a of the German Grundgesetz.

Against the students and the future decision makers at all levels the university commits itself to play a pioneering role for sustainability, particularly in the daily operations such as the sustainable use of energy and other natural resources.

B. Guidelines

1. The university supports discussions on the concept of sustainability and promotes a broad participation of all stakeholders inside the university in that process. The university also strengthens all internal initiatives and commitments und promotes the exchange of groups and institutions on the regional, national and international level.

2. The forums and institutions of the university support disciplinary and interdisciplinary projects in research, teaching and training and any activities from the administration and the students that address sustainability issues.
3. The researchers and scientists of the university are being encouraged to devote their research activities to sustainability issues.
4. The university welcomes proposals of the faculties for additional courses on sustainability and on the integration of issues on sustainability into curricula and courses.
5. The university enables university employees both on the scientific and non-scientific level to use education and training on sustainability issues.
6. The university supports initiatives for the development of new forms of knowledge transfer that can strengthen sustainable development and the transdisciplinary exchange.
7. The university is responsible to minimize the consumption of energy and natural resources and to create environmentally sound and less risky conditions for its own operations.

C. Decisions of the university on sustainability

Since 1997, the University of Lüneburg has undertaken the following actions in the pursue of sustainable development:
- Participation in the COPERNICUS Programme of the Association of European Universities (CRE) on the basis of the University Charta for Sustainable Development
- Decision of the senate on the establishment of a specialized commission entitled "University and Agenda 21" in conjunction with the appointment of a designated official for Agenda 21
- Decision of the senate on research priorities such as "Environmental Quality and Biodiversity" and "Agenda 21"
- Decision of the senate on "Environmental Principles at the University of Lüneburg"

The Guidelines for Sustainability were adopted by the senate of the University of Lüneburg on 17 May 2000.

References

Bundesministerium für Bildung und Forschung (BMBF; 2002): Report of the Federal Government on Education for Sustainable Development, Bonn.
Ev. Akademie Loccum (1997): Thesen, Materialien und überarbeitete Beiträge des Kolloquiums "Hochschule, nachhaltige Entwicklung und die Agenda 21" vom 11./12.11.1997.
Kuckartz, U. (1996): Ökologisierung von Hochschulen, Berlin.
Leal, W./MacDermott, F./Padgham, J. (1996): Implementing Sustainable Development at University Level; Bradford.
Michelsen, G. (Hrsg.; 2000): Sustainable University. Auf dem Weg zu einem universitären Agendaprozess. Frankfurt a.M.
Runder Tisch Agenda 21: Zwischenbericht des Runden Tisches zum Dialogprozess Agenda 21 in Niedersachsen, o.Ersch.Verm.
Stoltenberg, U./Michelsen, G. (1999): Lernen nach der Agenda 21: Überlegungen zu einem Bildungskonzept für eine nachhaltige Entwicklung, in: NNA-Berichte, 12. Jg, H. 1, Schneverdingen, S. 45-54.

Emanuel Rogier van Mansvelt

The Dutch Example: a Bottom-up Approach to Integrating Sustainable Development in Higher Education

Introduction

Modern society is complex and subject to rapid change. This implies a desparate need for knowledge and skills, not only for today's citizens, but also for future generations. The skills needed include the ability to communicate across the borders of sectors and disciplines, to understand the coherence between processes and to analyse their trends. In addition to knowledge such skills are needed to find an answer to the question: 'What is needed to realise a society that is more sustainable than the present one?'

Sustainable development as it is described in the UN Brundtland report in 1987 *'development that meets the needs of the present without compromising the ability of future generations to meet their own needs'* (World Commission on Environment and Development 1987) asks for an approach in which economic, social and ecological aspects are integrated and which not only focuses on today but also on tomorrow and beyond.

The need for new skills implies important challenges for universities and institutions for higher education. More focus on complexity and the competences to deal with complexity are needed in addition to more disciplinary oriented knowledge.

In the Netherlands considerations like those given above have led to, among others, the formation of a network that aims to stimulate higher education to face these new challenges and to improve the quality of education. The vision of this network is that in the Netherlands all graduates of higher education should have learned how to contribute to sustainable development. The network defined five priority areas. In the first place, all study programs should, at the onset of the program, make students familiar with the basics of sustainable development such as the coherence between social, ecological and economic aspects. In addition to that, students should learn how they can contribute to sustainable development from the perspective of their own discipline. All students should, towards the end of their study, co-operate with fellow students from other disciplines in an interdisciplinary research project related to sustainable development. Furthermore universities should create opportunities for specialising in sustainable development by offering a broad range of courses and a Master programme on sustainable development. As a result of this approach in higher education all graduates should be able to incorporate aspects of sustainable development in their future work.

Of course the approach described above is a very ambitious one and we have to say that till now of all students and teachers in the Netherlands only about 5 % actively participate in the network. However, the results so far are most promising and stimulating. They also make clear, as will be described below, that student participation can play a very important role.

In this chapter we will describe how the Dutch network on sustainable development in higher education is organised, but before doing that we will give an overview of its development so far. Therefore the next paragraph goes back in time to 1995 describing how students expressed their concerns on the fact that universities were not actively implementing the COPERNICUS Charter on sustainable development and collaboratively took action. Subsequently we will describe how the network is organised today and what the plans are for the future. Some examples of current projects will be given as well.

Bottom-up Approach Creates a Spin-off

In 1995 students within several Dutch universities organised themselves in student groups to stimulate the environmental management of physical operations. In those early days students mainly focused on items like energy reduction, treatment of chemical waste, introduction of environmentally friendly coffee cups and the use of recycled paper. In order to learn from each other student groups from different universities formed the Dutch National Environmental Student Platform (LHUMP). A year later students started to organise activities aiming at the integration of sustainable development aspects in the curricula. In 1998 the student platform developed into the present Dutch Network for Higher Education and Sustainable Development.

What Happened after Signing the COPERNICUS Charter?

In autumn 1995, a student active in the LHUMP found out that the rectors of all Dutch universities (except one) had signed the COPERNICUS Charter. By signing the charter universities formally agree to integrate sustainable development in education, research and operational management. The students were particularly interested in actions in relation to action point 4 of the COPERNICUS Charter:

> *Universities shall incorporate an environmental perspective in all their work and set up environmental education programmes involving both teachers and researchers as well as students – all of whom should be exposed to the global challenge of environment and development, irrespective of their field of study* (COPERNICUS Charter).

It was not so clear, however, what had been realised in practices after signing the Charter. Therefore LHUMP decided to send a letter to all university boards inquiring on what had been done after signing.

Only two universities responded. One university wanted to know more about the charter they had signed – the COPERNICUS Charter was send to this university –, and the other responded that not much had been done yet. A month later the boards of the universities that had not responded were approached by telephone with again the question what had been done after signing the Charter in 1993. LHUMP started to publish a newsletter (on recycled paper) with an update of the integration of sustainable development in the curricula of Dutch universities. The newsletter was distributed to university boards, faculty deans, curricula committees, national organisations involved in quality assessment, to the Ministry of Education, Culture and Research and to the Ministry of Health, Spatial Planning and Environment. LHUMP also organised national meetings and a conference during which a European wide study on the results of the COPERNICUS Charter performed by one of the students was presented (Doctor and Pesschier 1995).

Although the first initiative to spread information on integration of sustainable development into higher education curricula came from students thereby taking the first steps towards a network, some teachers and staff members had been performing small-scale individual initiatives and were happy with an emerging platform. Others were newly inspired. Some universities, like Utrecht University and the University of Nijmegen, installed comities on the implementation of the COPERNICUS Charter. Of course a change within the university system is not easily brought about and the results were often disappointing for the students active in LHUMP. For instance, in Nijmegen a report first 'dissappeard' in bureaucratic structures, but later on the recommendations made in the report were implemented; pressure by active students certainly was an important factor in the process. At the University of Nijmegen a COPERNICUS co-ordinator was employed to work out the recommendations of the report and nowadays, Nijmegen is one of the leading universities on education for sustainable development.

At Utrecht University the committee on implementation of the COPERNICUS Charter decided not to develop earth shattering plans to give shape to the principle actions included in the COPERNICUS Charter (Filho 1996). The committee stated that a lot of the areas of Agenda 21 (Agenda 21, 1992) were already covered by research activities. No concrete plans were made to integrate sustainable development in regular study programmes. The committee chose the point of view that students who wanted to learn about environmental aspects should choose to study environmental sciences and therefore the COPERNICUS initiative within Utrecht University has a strong link with study programmes related to environmental sciences.

Another example is the Technical University Delft where, because of the commitment of the university board, all faculties have the obligation to incorporate sustainable development aspects in all study programmes.

The LHUMP also started co-operation with students from other European countries in the framework of the International Students for Environmental Action (ISEA), which was later renamed Global Organisation of Students for Environmental Action (GOSEA; www.gosea.org). In 1996 ISEA recommended serious implementation of the COPERNICUS Charter by universities and in their actions they focussed on action point 4 of the Charter (see above) according to which every student, regardless of his or her study and interest, should become familiar, as far as possible or relevant, with the interrelatedness of his or her field of study and sustainable development (Jansen 1996).

The challenge was, and still is, to integrate sustainable development in all university curricula. To stimulate the process of integrating sustainable development in university curricula research projects on possibilities for integration of sustainable development aspects in specific disciplinary domains were set up. The first project was in the domain of general and business economy. The results of the study were published together with recommendations and suggestions for changing the curricula (see also the intermezzo's).

A Charter for Universities for Vocational Education

The COPERNICUS Charter was signed by all 14 universities in the Netherlands, but as the institutions for higher vocational education were not members of the European Rectors Conference (CRE, the cradle of the COPERNICUS Charter), about 60 Dutch institutions in the field of higher education were not amongst the signatories. Therefore LHUMP, in which university students and students from universities for vocational education were co-operating, stimulated the draft of a specific COPERNICUS charter for Dutch universities for vocational education. As will be evident from the preceding section, a weak point of the COPERNICUS Charter is that there is no obligation for the signatories to practise what the Charter preaches, what in practise too often means that after signing the Charter nothing happens. This weak point was given much attention by the LHUMP initiated activities in the field of vocational higher education. The drafted document has a great degree of resemblance to the European COPERNICUS charter, but the Dutch COPERNICUS Charter for universities of vocational education is accompanied by a Protocol and both documents have to be signed not only by the university board, but also by faculty deans and operational management. During the process a manager of one of the universities for vocational education took over the LHUMP initiative and managed to motivate the 30 largest institutions for higher vocational education to sign both the Charter and the Protocol. Presently some universities for vocational education who signed that Charter and Protocol are way ahead of universities which signed the European COPERNICUS charter. Implementation of the Protocol is co-ordinated by a consultancy organisation which assesses the curricula of the universities who signed the Protocol. Universities who implemented all guidelines and conditions described in the Protocol are certified and every two years a new and more strict protocol is written.

An Award for Sustainable Development in Higher Education

In 1997 a 'debate tour' through the Netherlands was organized by the scientific bureau of the Dutch labour party. The LHUMP tried successfully to integrate a debate on the COPERNICUS Charter in the tour. That debate took place in Maastricht, and amongst the discussion partners were one of the rectors that had been involved in drafting the COPERNICUS charter, a student and the minister of education. At the end of the debate that minister launched an award for sustainable development in higher education curricula. From both universities and universities for vocational education an impressive amount of existing 'sustainable'curricula and plans for transforming curricula were submitted and in June 1998 an event was organised to present the winners and their future plans.

During this event the idea came up to organise a national conference on the integration of sustainable development in higher education and half a year later, in December 1998, the University of Amsterdam and LHUMP organised such a conference together. In several workshops concrete plans for actions to support good initiatives at different institutions were discussed and at the end of the day four projects were agreed upon (see intermezzo's 1, 2, 3 and 4). First of all, a steering committee consisting of motivated individuals from LHUMP, universities, universities for vocational education, and ministries was formed. This steering committee has the task to co-ordinate activities and to operate as a clearing house for new ideas and information. Secondly, a project to take up interdisciplinary study modules in the curricula was developed. These modules are real-case projects on problems related to sustainable development in society (see intermezzo's 1 and 2). Thirdly, a 'teaching the teachers for sustainable development' project was initiated (see intermezzo 3). The last component in the action plan was the development of criteria to measure and assess sustainable development in higher education (see intermezzo 4).

That first conference resulted in the formation of a network in which students, teachers and policy makers worked together on the common objective to integrate sustainable development in higher education. Since that time a series of conferences on a range of themes has been organised. Some students who were active in LHUMP joined the network as professionals after graduation. Presently the Dutch network is growing steadily and is linking different actors. More than one hundred teachers and full-time employed university staff members and about five hundred people working on a part-time basis are involved.

Organisation of the Dutch Network for Sustainable Development in Higher Education

As was described in the previous sections, the Dutch network for sustainable development in higher education started bottom-up with students and teachers who motivated people at universities, ministries and NGO's to join. Today the network consists of a wide variety of motivated people: students, university board members, staff and NGO's all motivated to contribute to changing education in such a way that sustainable development is integratd in all curricula.

The network is co-ordinated by the Steering Committee for Higher Education for Sustainable Development (CDHO). Members of the Steering Committee are students, university board members, project co-ordinators (see the intermezzo's) and individuals working at the Ministry of Health, Planning and Environment, the Ministry of Education, Culture and Science, The Ministry of Economic Affairs and the Ministry of Agriculture, Nature and Fishery. The members of the Steering Committee are participating on an individual basis and do not represent their organisation in a formal way. The Steering Committee initiates activities and promotes the exchange of knowledge between universities, ministries and NGO's both at a national and at an international level. Universities are stimulated to incorporate sustainable development in their mission, policy plans, and all their curricula. Closer co-operation between civil organisations, higher education institutions and ministries on sustainable development issues is stimulated. As a result of this approach the importance of higher education for sustainable development is mentioned in several government policy documents and about half a million Euro per year is received from governmental resources.

The CDHO organises projects in which different institutions for higher education participate. Examples of such projects are 'Interdisciplinary education', 'North-South', 'Challenging experts' and 'Quality assessment and quality control for sustainable development in higher education', 'Sustainable multiple area use at universities', 'Long term thinking and higher education for sustainable development', 'A Master programme in sustainable development'. A description of some projects and their results is given in the intermezzo's in this chapter.

The Steering Committee is supported by a small secretariat, supporting existing projects and initiating new ones. The secretariat functions as a clearing house for all the project outputs and organises communication through the – still existing – COPERNICUS-newsletter, a website (www.dho21.nl), emaillist and library with an on-line catalog. The secretariat organises a yearly national network meeting and has contacts with a great number of national and international organisations.

Intermezzo 1: Interdisciplinary Education

The aim of the project 'Interdisciplinary education' is to give students working for their master degree the opportunity to participate in an interdisciplinary research program related to sustainable development aspects. This research project is situated in a real life setting in society. The objective is the training of competences needed to work on complex societal problems. This implies both the involvement of people with different disciplinary backgrounds and different actors from society.

The educational model is developed by the teachers participating in the project. Students with different disciplinary backgrounds and studying at different higher education institutions, form the research team. The general set-up of the case is outlined clearly in a base document. Starting from this document the students have to formulate their own research proposal with consensus of all students participating. The teacher functions as a coach for the research team.

The students work full-time on the project for a period of 14 weeks and have to respect a tight time schedule. In the first week the date for the presentation of the research proposal is set, the concept of the report is drafted and the date for the final presentation and evaluation report is determined. No delay is accepted.

The students are supposed to get several parties engaged in their research activities. These parties include companies, citizens-organizations, NGO's and local or national governments relevant for the project. During the project the students recognize conflicting interests and values that come into prominence when working on sustainable development in a real life situation. All parties are invited for the final presentation and their comments on the report presented are taken into account in the final assessment of the students.

The results until now show that this education model is an excellent method for students to learn about sustainable development. But the benefits are not just for the students, also recommendations for actual improvements within society are a result of these projects. It is a rewarding job to motivate, engage and prepare students for sustainable development in their future role in society. The Dutch network is willing to support universities interested in this education model and is interested in working together with universities all over the world to organize these kinds of projects together. The North-South project outline in intermezzo 2 describes interdisciplinary projects between universities in all continents of the world.

Intermezzo 2: North-South, Student Projects on Sustainable Development in Asia, Africa, and Latin America

As sustainable development is a worldwide process, intercultural co-operation is essential. Such an approach, and the continuous challenge for poverty alleviation without ecological destruction is currently experienced as a very important challenge by scientists, politicians, and other leading parties in the world. At the same time this challenge is considered as an extremely complicated and difficult one. The North-South project wants to educate future generations of scientists and politicians and equip them with better skills than most members of the present generation have for finding a balance between poverty alleviation on the one hand and fighting environmental degradation on the other. Therefore a central question is can sustainable development be realised via intercultural co-operation based on equity and using the creativity of different continents?

The North-South project has been established in January 2001. It is based on the vision that actual experience is the best way to equip students with the skills indicated above. Students participate in a multi-disciplinary, intercultural research team in Africa, Asia or Latin America for a local organization on sustainable development. The research takes place in collaboration with a local university.

The project takes experiential learning and a student-oriented form of education as starting points. The interdisciplinary educational model, described in intermezzo 1, is used as the basic methodology. In the research groups about 6 to 8 Master's students from different disciplines participate. Half of the students are from the Netherlands, the other half are from the country in which the research activities takes place. The research is carried out in close collaboration with a non-university organization (a local NGO, governmental organization or company). The focus of the research is always defined by the local organization. The outcome of the project generates concrete recommendations that are practically applicable and have direct local relevance. This means that they must be socially acceptable, and technically and economically feasible.

The research project incorporates the following aspects of sustainable development:
- Future-oriented; the research is directed at solutions not only for the present, but also for the long term;
- Ecological aspects; the research wants to contribute to the improvement of the ecological situation or to fight ecological damage to the environment in both short and long term;
- Economic aspects; the research aims at improving the living conditions of people in the South;
- Social aspects; the research aims at the improvement of social structures (gender issues, equity, democracy) and wants to avoid developments that are socially undesirable.

In general, students and other stakeholders are very positive about the North-South initiative. Spring 2002, the first student groups have finished their research projects. An earlier pilot-project has shown that students learn most effectively in cross-cultural settings if there is a certain balance in skills and age. However, these experiences are still rather new. After a second project year the experiences in these interdisciplinary, intercultural projects can be used to improve the method and set up similar projects with interested partners. All teachers, universities or stakeholders interested to set up similar projects are invited to share experiences and contact us (www.northe-south.org, northe-south@dho21.nl).

Intermezzo 3: Challenging Experts

The aim of the project is to explore the relations between various disciplines and sustainable development, and to challenge teachers and university boards to integrate sustainable development into all disciplinary study programmes.

Generally speaking, university lecturers are experts in their fields and do not like to follow training programmes, certainly not when these programmes are obligatory and imposed by authorities. Moreover, teachers do not have much time to explore new areas outside their own discipline. It should be mentioned, however, that university lecturers are usually quite well informed about the most recent developments within their own discipline, partly because of the direct relation between education and research. The best way to motivate lecturers and researchers therefore is to refer to their field of expertise, and to present sustainable development as an intellectual challenge in their field. For that reason teachers in specific disciplines were invitesd to describe the challenges of integrating sustainable development in the education in their own field in a review of about fifty pages. The review must also contain recommendations for changing education. After the completion of a review seminars are organised for colleagues from the faculty and from other universities. At these seminars the reviews are presented and recommendations are discussed.

During the process of writing disciplinary reviews and during the seminars many people become involved. Often interviews with colleage experts from other institutions create the basis for the review. In addition to the review, valuable strategic lessons can be derived as a result of the process.

So far the folowing reviews have been published:
Business management (Jonker and Grollers, 2001); *Economics* (van den Bergh and Withagen, 2001); *Physics* (Bras-Klapwijk, 2001); *History* (van Zon, 2001); *Biology* (van Hengstum, 2001) and *Mathematics* (Alberts, 2001).

The experiences of the past two years led to a number of recommendations incorporated in the 'Challenging experts plan of action'. This plan of action is a practical method for institutions and lecturers wishing to work towards the integration of the concept of sustainable development in education through the development of 'disciplinary reviews'. It can be viewed on www.dho21.nl/english/reviews.

Intermezzo 4: Quality Assessment and Quality Control for Sustainable Development in Higher Education

During the first network meeting in December 1998 a project on the development of criteria for sustainable development in higher education was agreed upon. An instrument was developed and tested in the Netherlands and in Sweden. At the beginning of 2002 the Auditing Instrument for Sustainable Higher Education (AISHE) was officially launched (Roorda 2001).

The AISHE instrument is based on the EFQM model (European Foundation for Quality Management). This model for quality improvement is an iterative process: plan, do, and check. The AISHE instrument covers important steps for the integration of sustainable development in higher education: creating a vision; communication about sustainable development; curricula guidelines; the method of teaching; interdisciplinary approach; examination and evaluation. The main focus of the AISHE instrument is education. To audit physical operations, good instruments are available like EMAS and ISO 14001.

The AISHE instrument is used as follows. A study co-ordinator or manager organizes two meetings lasting each about 4 hours. One or two managers, about ten teachers, three students and one or two key persons directly involved with education, all of the same discipline or study participate these sessions. During the first meeting a consultant will introduce higher education for sustainable development and explain the way the AISHE instrument works. Then all participants examine the criteria individually. Each criterion has five stages, beginning from almost nothing happening to an integrated vision on the matter.

The second meeting is the consensus meeting. All individual scores are put together so students can see what the managers scored and vice versa. All criteria are discussed one at the time. The chair is a trained AISHE consultant who tries to achieve consensus on each criterion.

After a consensus is agreed on the present situation, the desired situation for the next two or three years will be explored. At the end of the discussion about the desired situation a list is created with concrete ideas and proposals for increasing quality of education for sustainable development.

In 2002, the 'AISHE project' aims to audit about 15 curricula at higher education institutions. Besides auditing all different kinds of disciplines the aim of the project is to train consultants who will be able to audit study programs at their own universities. The AISHE instrument is available in English and can be used freely by any university. An additional aim of the AISHE project is to integrate AISHE criteria in the regular Dutch quality assessments of higher education. Presently in Europe new bodies for accreditation are launched; it would be most useful if sustainable development would be among the guidelines for accreditation of existing and new curricula.

The AISHE audit leaves the institute with a good overview of sustainable development and it drafts an outline for creating a curriculum contributing to sustainable development. The AISHE audit instrument is free of publishing rights and therefore free to use. The initiators are interested to learn if people are inspired to use the instrument or want more information about AISHE.

References

Alberts (2001): Wiskunde & duurzame ontwikkeling, Netwerk Duurzaam Hoger Onderwijs, Nijmegen.
Agenda 21(1992): UNCED – United Nations Conference on Environment and Development.
Bergh, J. van den en Withagen, C. (2001): Economie & duurzame ontwikkeling, Netwerk Duurzaam Hoger Onderwijs, Amsterdam.

Brundtland Commission (1979): Our Common Futures, Report of the World Commission on Environment and Development, Oxford University Press. New York.

Bras - Klapwijk, R. (2001): Natuurkunde & duurzame ontwikkeling, Netwerk Duurzaam Hoger onderwijs, Delft.

Doctor, L./Peschier, M. (1995): The Integration of sustainable development in education and research at universities in Europe. Wageningen Agricultural University, Wageningen.

Hengstum, G. van (2001): Biologie & duurzame ontwikkeling, Netwerk Duurzaam Hoger Onderwijs, Nijmegen.

Jonker, J./Grollers, R. (2001): Bedrijfskunde & duurzame ontwikkeling, Netwerk Duurzaam Hoger Onderwijs, Nijmegen.

Filho, W.L./MacDermott, F./Padgham, J. (1996): Implementing sustainable development at university life. A Manual of good practice. CRE-Copernicus. University of Bradfort, Bradford.

Roorda, N. (2001): Auditing Instrument for Sustainability in Higher Education (AISHE). University of Amsterdam, Amsterdam.

World Commission on Environment and Development (1987): Our Common Future. Oxford University Press: Oxford.

Zon, H. van (2002): Geschiedenis & duurzame ontwikkeling, Netwerk Duurzaam Hoger Onderwijs, Griningen.

Heloise Buckland, Fiona Brookes, Deborah Seddon, Andy Johnston, Sara Parkin

The UK Higher Education Partnership for Sustainability (HEPS)

Box Quote: Taking a holistic approach to universities and colleges and encouraging the integration of activities on campus in the curriculum and with the community to achieve sustainable development is at the heart of the Higher Education Partnership for Sustainability.

The Higher Education Partnership for Sustainability (HEPS) is a partnership of 18 United Kingdom Higher Education Institutions committed to sustainability, involved in a 3-year project co-ordinated by Forum for the Future, the leading UK sustainable development charity. The mission of the HEPS is "to establish a pioneering partnership group of Higher Education (HE) institutions that are seen to be achieving strategic objectives through positive engagement with the sustainable development agenda and to generate the transferable tools, guidance and the inspiration that will encourage the rest of the sector to do likewise."

HEPS has now come to the end of its first fully operational year. Throughout 2001 we have been recruiting partners, carrying out opening sustainability reviews, preparing for a series of partnership wide seminars in the autumn term and undertaking individual work with partners.

The HEPS does not prescribe a model of a sustainable university and recognises that every institution has its own unique character. In pursuit of real, long term change driven from within, the HEPS identifies specific objectives and helps the institutions achieve them in the most sustainable way. Enabling partners to be leaders in the field is given a high priority by this initiative, but so too is sharing the learning and experience of the HEPS within – and beyond – the HE sector.

The HEPS builds on the existing good practice accumulated by the HE21 project, draws upon the expertise and networks of Forum for the Future's work in other sectors and the learning methodologies and feedback gained through the Masters programme in Leadership for Sustainable Development run by Forum for the Future.

HE21 Project – Best Practice in Higher Education

HE21 was a Forum for the Future led project aimed at accumulating best practice in the Higher Education sector. Partner institutions were consulted on a number of issues including biodiversity, resource efficiency, community learning, waste minimisation, purchasing, transport and environmental management systems. A series of best practice bulletins were produced and are available to download at www.heps.org.uk. Two major conferences were also held to showcase best practice and build partnerships for the future.

Forum for the Future – Knowledge, Experience and Networks across Sectors

Forum for the Future also works in partnership with decision-makers in business and local and regional government and the HEPS draws upon the experiences and expertise of colleagues working in these partnerships. The HEPS has links with the construction sector through Forum's Business Programme, has used culture change techniques developed by Forum's Local and Regional Government Programme and is working with the communications experts of the Forum magazine *Green Futures* to develop promotional material. More details of Forum for the Future are available at www.forumforthefuture.org.uk and you can subscribe to Green Futures at www.greenfutures.org.uk.

The Scholarship Programme – Masters in Leadership for Sustainable Development

Designed by Forum's Programme Director, Sara Parkin, this is a one year full time masters course which emphasises work-based, experiential learning as well as reflection and cutting edge sustainability knowledge. The programme is run by Forum for the Future and validated by Middlesex University and is in its 6th year. Throughout the programme there are clear Learning Outcomes to achieve and the three core elements of the programme are:
- Interactive and practical seminars to develop leadership, reflective practice and other transferable skills
- Tuition from leading experts in sustainable development in four key themes covering science, economics, ethics and values, society and the community.
- One month placements in organisations in six key sectors of UK society; an NGO environment or development campaigning organisation, local or regional government, UK or European politics, a leading business, a regulatory or financial institution and the media.

The HEPS draws on the learning techniques and experiences gained from the placements so far in over 130 organisations in the above six sectors. In particular this provides insight into graduate skills needed by employers as well as first hand up to date experience of how these key sectors are contributing towards sustainable development.

What are the Key Objectives of the HEPS?

The following are the key objectives of the HEPS, against which progress is measured throughout the course of the programme:
- To embed a strategic approach to sustainable development into partner institutions.

- To create a sense of common purpose and leadership amongst the partner institutions, to better influence the sector-wide change.
- To design a web-based system for Sustainability Reporting for HEIs that has broad support in the sector and is consistent with best practice within the sector (e.g. HE Sustainability Measures) and beyond it (e.g. Global Reporting Initiative for business). It will also be consonant with government policy (e.g. Sustainability Indicators).
- To leave senior management in partner institutions with the knowledge, motivation and skills to structure sustainability into the university's strategic and operational planning processes, research policies, and curriculum planning.
- To build similar capacity in the HEI's stakeholder community – business partners, local and regional government, funding councils and other associated organisations, research councils, students, suppliers.
- To complete a number of innovative partner-designated initiatives that drive forward the agenda, demonstrating clear benefits.
- To develop materials and processes which are communicated and shared with partners and others.

Who are the Organisations Involved?

The HEPS is a partnership between the following 18 universities and colleges and Forum for the Future. It is supported by the Funding Councils of England, Northern Ireland, Scotland and Wales. The funds being made available over the 3 years total over £750,000.

- University of Aberdeen
- Heriot-Watt University
- University of Birmingham
- University of Brighton
- University of Cambridge
- City University
- University of St Andrews
- University of Stirling
- Middlesex University
- University of Newcastle
- University of Salford
- Sheffield Hallam University

- Liverpool John Moores University
- The Surrey Institute of Art & Design
- Loughborough University
- College of St Mark & St John
- Queens University, Belfast
- Cardiff University

Each participating institution is contracted to bring to the partnership 'in-kind' contributions amounting to at least £10,000 per year. This includes staff time and the use of facilities for meetings and events. This brings the total value of the scheme to over £1.47 million.

How does it work in practice?

The overall direction of the HEPS is steered by a group of representatives from universities, funding councils, the national student body, the private sector, regional government and Forum for the Future. Commitment to active engagement in the universities is agreed at the Vice-Chancellor or Principal level, with overall management residing with a member of the senior management team.

The HEPS has two strategies to promote sector wide change by working closely with the institutions to help them achieve their objectives in a sustainable way and also to influence a broad spectrum of other key stakeholders.

Driving change from within

The programme for each partner institution begins with an Opening Sustainability Review to assess expectations about the partnership in order to design a work programme tailored to the strategic objectives of the institution. Representatives from the senior management team, operational staff, academics and students attend this one-day event. The review reflects on the role of universities and colleges as:

- institutions which form and inform tomorrow's (and today's) leaders and decision-makers through teaching and research agendas;
- managers of major businesses where prudent use of resources not only saves money but safeguards reputations;
- important actors in local communities and regional development – as employer, purchaser, service user and provider.

The work programme is then delivered through three types of activities:

- Individual Work Programmes – Individual initiatives are identified by each institution and the HEPS team help facilitate these through background research, networking, report writing and visits to the institution.
- Partnership Wide Initiatives – The HEPS partners identified a number of key themes to be addressed by all. For each theme the HEPS undertakes research, holds workshops for the partners, organises seminars for the sector and other key players and finally produces appropriate guidance to build the capacity to accelerate sector wide change.
- Sustainability Reporting – The HEPS is developing a framework and process for tracking progress and communicating outcomes on key sustainability issues. This will enable each institution to measure and communicate its own progress towards sustainability. Research and seminars will be held in 2002 to develop this area of work with the intention of a web-based sustainability reporting system to be available by the end of 2003.

Influencing the external forces

The HEPS has identified several key external players including funding councils, other arms of government, Professional Associations, Trade Unions, research councils and other funders, auditors and assessors. The HEPS team are building up a bank of key contacts within each of these organisations to monitor their activities, involve them in the HEPS where appropriate and influence policy where possible. A recent outcome of this is the HEPS involvement in developing a framework for the new sustainable development strategy group which the Professional Associations for Higher Education have agreed to set up.

What has HEPS Achieved so far?

Opening Sustainability Reviews

A day has been spent in all 18 partner institutions with representatives from senior management, estates, academic and administrative arms to introduce the concept of sustainable development, identify the institution's key drivers and barriers to contributing towards sustainable development and highlight potential areas of work with the HEPS.

Individual work programmes

Each institution has selected a few key themes to develop individually through the HEPS and these are highlighted in the grid overleaf. In areas of common interest clusters are forming to share experiences across the partnership. City University, Middlesex University and the Surrey Institute of Art and Design (all located in the South East of England) recently convened to share their experiences of using various techniques being developed by the HEPS to embed sustainable development into their strategic planning processes. Partners have also expressed interest in forming clusters to work on staff development, waste management and identifying the key drivers for a University or College to contribute towards sustainable development.

Translating Theory into Practice

	Surrey Institute of A & D	University of Stirling	University of St Andrews	Sheffield Hallam University	University of Salford	Queen's University Belfast	University of Newcastle	Middlesex University	College of St Mark & St John	Loughborough University	L'pool John Moores University	Heriot-Watt University	City University	Cardiff University	University of Cambridge	University of Birmingham	University of Brighton	University of Aberdeen	
Strategic planning	■			■					■				■		■	■		■	Business
Sustainability audit			■																Business
Transport					■					■									Business
Energy	■			■															Business
Resource efficiency (waste)														■					Business
Environmental plan													■			■			Business
Buildings (new, old, BREAM)					■	■			■							■			Business
Sustainable Procurement						■										■			Business
Whole life costing					■														Business
Changing corporate culture								■											Learning & research
Student energising		■																	Learning & research
Staff development																■			Learning & research
Environmetnal education																			Learning & research
Curriculum development		■		■		■			■		■					■			Learning & research
Curriculum new programme						■		■											Learning & research
Research agenda development									■										Learning & research
Research drivers for SD in HE																			Learning & research
Community liasion	■				■														Community
Working with local businesses	■													■					Community
Communication strategy									■										Community
Urban Regeneration				■															Community

Partnership wide initiatives

Sustainable procurement, construction and travel have been addressed this year and the following has been achieved;

Theme	Research	Outcomes	Future work
Construction	Desk research of partners and regulators policies and practices.	2 workshops for HEPS partners 2 seminars for wider audience	Developing guidance on sustainable construction for new build and refurbishment. Considering position statement to build consensus on the issues.
Travel	Questionnaires completed by partners to identify policy and practice.	2 workshops for HEPS partners 2 seminars with exhibitions for wider audience	Developing guidance on how to promote sustainable travel across an institution with future integration into Resource Management initiative.
Procurement	Telephone interviews undertaken.	Workshop for HEPS partners procurement officers.	Developing guidance for sustainable procurement and future integration into Finance initiative.

The events above were attended by approximately 200 delegates from the HEPS partners (with representatives from senior management, estates, academics, administration, students and local community) other Higher Education Institutions, funding councils, local government, business, experts in the field, consultants, practitioners and others.

Plans for 2002

The individual work programmes will continue in each institution with a greater degree of 'clustering' and the major themes to be addressed partnership wide are sustainable resource management, finance, communication and sustainability reporting. Details of these initiatives will be posted on www.heps.org.uk in January 2002 and there will be a number of seminars open to all interested parties.

Conclusions

The greatest challenge so far in delivering the HEPS is the lack of available resources within each institution to progress initiatives hence the continual emphasis on helping the institutions achieve their existing strategic objectives in a sustainable way rather than creating 'extra work'. The most successful aspect of the programme to date is the momentum gained through sharing and consensus building across the partnership and beyond.

Box Quote: If we are serious about sustainability, then it is the decision-makers of the immediate future we need to target urgently. However important it may be that the right knowledge and skills are stitched into every aspect of our education system, our priority is the people who will be in leadership roles in the next 5 to 10 years.

Piera Ciceri, Camilla Bargellini, Fausta Setti

A Network of Knowledge and Practices for Sustainability: an Italian Project Linking University, School System and Local Community through Participation to Agenda 21 Processes

The context

Our project has its roots within the more general context of the recent evolution of global and local economic, social, political, environmental and cultural scenarios and of the ever increasing awareness of an undelayable reorientation of development towards more sustainable approaches.

The definition of what can be meant in practice by "sustainable development" is not univocal, but has to be the resultant of a continual process, involving at different levels all social stakeholders, representing goals and interests of governments, local authorities, enterprises, academia, consumers, NGOs, media and other actors.

In a society that wants to be democratic, such an involvement has to be planned and realised, both as responsibilities for managing our social and natural environment are collective and personal ones, and as governance decisions need to be fully acquired and accepted by the whole community in order to be effective, resulting from changes in consumption, production patterns, behaviours and lifestyles.

Local Agenda 21 represents the framework and the tool for local governments to engage in implementing the outcomes of the United Nations Conference on Environment and Development (Rio de Janeiro 1992). Key element of it is participation, where local stakeholders collaborate to define a shared vision of their community development, to identify proposals and priorities for action, to assess local social, economic and environmental conditions and needs, to negotiate targets and to monitor procedures.

However, in order to plan and to participate to this process, all actors need to possess adequate competences and abilities, beyond the specific ones of their usual professional role, such as those pertaining to the relational domain and implying finding common languages, negotiation, listening and respecting other ideas, collaborative learning and working, etc. Competences and skills that have to be acquired both trough formal training and practice and that have to be accompanied by a parallel long-life process of education of all individuals, so to promote the rising and the rooting of an active and responsible citizenship in all members of a community.

The role of the educational system

Within the process of defining goals and actions towards sustainability, the educational system is charged of carrying out many tasks at different levels together with all other social actors in order to:
- create a new relationship between education system and its local community, so to represent a real resource for the definition and implementation of sustainable projects within the territory. Actually, as in the rest of Europe, in Italy too an increasing number of schools participate actively to projects promoted by their municipalities and devoted to better the quality of life of children and youngsters, to monitor pollution parameters of their fresh waters, to restore a local park, and the like;
- collaborate to the development of a long-life co-ordinated training process, in order to grant a continual professional updating and re-qualification of individuals, according to the evolving requests of a sustainable social and economic development. Italian high

schools and universities are slolwly moving in this direction, organizing specific graduate, post-graduate and other training courses for already employed people on topics ranging from production activities with respect to the environment to management of participatory processes for implementing Local A21 or to ISO or EMAS audit for enterprises and public institutions;
- contribute to develop in students awareness towards social and environmental issues, properly using the different tools offered by disciplines to analyze and interpretate reality, to responsibly choose among possible solutions, according to collective or individual values systems, and bringing them to acquire sense of belonging to their community and motivation to participate to its management. Environmental topics are the most chosen ones in Italian primary and secondary schools, allowing a transversal approach to real and complex problems of their own community, the integration of knowledge with eventual actions for their solution and the creation of networks of schools which operate under the coordination of environmental public and private agencies.
- cooperate in pre-service and in-service teacher training to have teachers acquire and increase their professionality with updated knowledge, learning contexts and methodologies more suitable to conform the school system to the new role it may play for the sustainable development of its community and for the new relational competences both teachers and students need in order to be effectively involved in participatory processes. In this respect, the Italian situation is still far from being adequate and the structural and organisational innovations which have been brought by during the last few years are not yet matched by significant reformation of the teacher training system, still based mainly on disciplinary contents and on a limited integration with psyco-pedagogical and didactic tools and methods. At present, pre-service teacher training for secondary lower and higher school levels is carried out by universities through a two year specialization course after the normal university degree in a specific disciplinary area, whereas in-service training is mainly offered by public and private agencies.

A21 as a challenge for the university system

In addition to the previous listed tasks, the university system –mainly in its scientific branches- has other fundamental roles of producing sound new knowledge, of contributing to its use in technological applications and to its "translation" into a language understandable by laymen.

Alltogether, the performance of such tasks should enable universities to give a significant support to sustainability and to local A21 processes, if it were not for its deeply rooted traditional isolation from the rest of society -particularly marked in the Italian situation- and for its evergrowing specialization in most fields, which is unapt to tackle complex systems like social and environmental ones, and which represents a psycological and cultural drawback for its researchers.

Our project

The main goal of our project is to provide primary and secondary schools with basic information, competence and tools, enabling them to be active promoters or participants either to Local A21 processes or to initiatives of some relevance oriented to a sustainable development of their community and realised with a participatory approach. In such a way, we mean to help schools and teachers in establishing a mutual relationship with their territory, up to now basically shifted toward the community being an active resource for the schools (as far as financial aid, data and experts are concerned), whereas schools are perceived only as a resource for educating "tomorrow citizens", but not relevant for present governance of their social and natural environment.

Being aware of the differences between goals and times of education and of governance, it is necessary that schools may be ready to engage themselves in a prolonged process, while finding opportunities to bring to an end (from planning to realisation) specific sub-projects with their classes.

In order to accomplish this goal, the choice of schools participating to our proposal has been restricted to already "advanced" situations and to equipe of teachers previously involved in our activities concerning environmental education and trans-disciplinary projects, trained to research and reflect on their professional competence.

Moreover, most schools are located in municipalities of limited dimensions and already oriented toward a sustainable development of their community, so as to facilitate the whole process.

The project is articulated on a two years basis and is organised in sequential phases, with initial strong emphasis on teacher training, followed by an engagement of local municipality and other social actors in order to identify a specific project and to realise it together with the schools, with final communication to the local community.

The teacher training process

The key-words which may better describe the training process are "collaborative and active learning", "flexible learning contexts" and "research approach".

This implies that participants will take active part in the building up of new skills, together with their colleagues, in a continual experimentation, sharing and reflection on their acquisitions, with possible requests of varying learning contents when needed by their practice, more according to a clinical approach than to a traditional transmissive one.

The first year of training will be devoted mainly to acquire information about Local A21, its phases and its typical tools for implementation. Working in groups, using role-playing, discussion, brainstorming, metaplan, telematic forums and other tools pertaining to methodologies of collaborative and distance learning, participants should improve their competence to analyse, understand and find solutions to problems, to manage group dynamics and conflicts, to dialogue with different auditors, to use basic communication tools. Moreover, such relational skills may well integrate disciplinary ones and could be applied and taught also to their students, as an opportunity to form them to present and future participation to school and community life.

One of the main phase during the first year of training is to have teachers carry out a preliminary analyses of their specific local context at three different levels: their own school, local municipality, other local stakeholders. in order to identify contacts with municipality and potential stakeholders to be involved in the setting of the specific project, to be carried out during the second phase of the training.

At school scale the request is to monitor existing kwnoledge about A21 and degree of interest for an eventual involvment in it, at municipality level to identify actual situation of the process, eventual priorities and referent subjects, so to be able to present a proposal which might be more "appealing" to local government. Thus, the suggested starting point for the analisys into the local community should be the existance of already established contacts, or projects or situations: that's what we name a recovery of previous "unconscious" Local Agenda 21 initiatives, whitout pretending from teachers an exhaustive monitoring of all local stakeholders and possible thematic areas of work.

The shift from simulation to reality will require during the second year a different training approach, which will be based mainly on a personalised coaching action, in order to accompany schools along the different steps of their project, supporting teachers to solve problems, to keep up their interactions with local authorities and experts, to organise activities with the class, and so on.
Strong event, initial "fuel" of the second part of the process, will be a workshop with teachers involved in the training process, their head

teachers and functionaires of their local municipalities. Experts in Local Agenda 21, functionaires presently working in successfull Local Agenda 21 processes and "facilitators" will manage work groups or forum, with the aim to show best practices and to dissolve fears, doubst, questions, needs of the partecipants.

Networking between participants will be granted by periodic meetings and by the telematic forum, in order to acquire new skills for participatory processes, improve old ones, share experiences, tools, reflections, identify possible interaction between different situations, define common tools to evaluate the learning process and their projects, organise the final co-operative report.

The co-ordination equipe of the training process

Five trainers are involved in planning and carrying on all activities pertaining to the project. They are all experts in teacher training and two of them hold a post-doctor position within the University of Milan.

This proposal is part of the activities of the Regional Centre for Environmental Education, which is run by the Biology Department of the University of Milan, under a contract with the government of the Lombardy region and with the financial support of the Italian Ministry of the Environment.

The training process has been accepted within projects for the Social European Fund by the Lombardy Region.

Notes after the first year

The first emerging critical point is the difficulty shown by teachers to shift from an environmental education project (even a "good" one) to a local Agenda 21 process. A lot of schools are actually able to ask support to their local authorities (economic or expert support) or are able to involve local community into their projects. Such projects, anyway, are usually totally defined from the schools themselves, mainly taking into consideration their educative goals and not also goals or interests of local municipality and other stakeholders. This ends up in local community representing a good resource for the school system, but only seldom in school system acting and being perceived by its community as a real resource at some level of governance of the territory and of its environmental problems.

The new approach requested to teachers needs to be supported by new skills, such as the ability to dialogue with different "languages", to negotiate with different legitimate interests, to confront with different times of action, to accept constraints of "real" situations.

During this first year of training role-playing, simulation activities, analyses of real case studies, discussions with different type of experts represented a significant learning context for the acquisition of such skills and supplied our participants with innovative tools for analysing their situation and defining a feasible project within a participatory approach.

The building of such context and type of projects requires a new thinking not only for teachers, but also for local authorities and it presents some problems in identifyng role and level of action each school might play in relation with its local situation. Obviously, an already well established process of Local Agenda 21 might facilitate a possible involvment of the school local system. Otherwise, schools have to try to play an active role in promoting the activation of the process. A role that, from our and other' experience, can be played almost exclusively in very small communities or in situations where the existance of a widespread and well rooted network of schools, already active on environmental projects relating to local problems, gives them legitimacy to advance proposals in such direction.

Outline of the training process

Participants
28 primary, lower and higher secondary schools of the Milan province.
Each school is represented by a team of teachers with humanistic and scientific competence, with the task of promoting methodologies and contents to the ampler group of colleagues which are involved in planning
and carrying out their specific school project.
In order to keep an adequate dimension for practical activities, participants have been divided into two parallel groups of about 25 teachers each, with common meetings for seminars and sharing in the telematic forum

Length
October 2001- June 2003

First year
- 35 hours for meetings in presence (seminars, working groups, discussions,..)
- 70 hours for team working and individual activities
- 15 hours for tutorial activities by the staff (face to face or via e-mail)

Contents
- goals, steps, tools and critical items of Local A21 processes
- survey of local situations and identification of feasible stekeholders, possibilities, areas of actions
- preliminary interactions with local authorities and stakeholders and setting of the project

Second year
- workshop with teachers, local authorities and head teachers
- 25 hours for meetings in presence
- estimated 100-200 hours/school for planning and realising class activities, team work and contacts with local partners
- 45 hours for tutorial activities by the staff
- diffusion of best practices

Contents
- planning and realising school projects
- organising communication activities
- evaluating the learning process and the projects
- writing intermediate and final reports

References

Alberti, M. (1998): Città, spazio ecologico e sostenibilità, Equilibri - rivista per lo sviluppo sostenibile, n.1, aprile/1998, Il Mulino/ Fondazione Enrico Mattei, Milano.

Altrichter, H./Kemmis, S./McTaggart, R./Zuber-Skerrit, O. (1991): Defining, Confining or Refining Action Research?, in: Zuber-Skerrit (a cura di), Action Research for Change and Development, Aldershot/Brookfield, Avebury.

ANPA (2000): Linee guida per le Agende 21 Locali, manual by Italian National Agency for Environmental Protection/Ambiente Italia.

AAVV (2000): Agenda 21 in classe, manual, C.R.E.A. Liguria.

Burton, P. (1993): Community Profiling. A guide to identifying local needs, University of Bristol, School of advanced Urban Studies.

Daniels, S.E./Walker, G.B. (1996): Collaborative learning: improving public deliberation in ecosystem-based management. Environmental impact assessment review, 16: 71–102.

Commissione dell'Unione Europea (1995): Insegnare e apprendere. Verso la società conoscitiva, Annali della Pubblica Istruzione, n.4 anno XLI, Le Monnier, Roma.

Elliot, J. (1991): Action Research for Educational Change, Open University Press, Milton Keynes.

European Foundation for the Improvement of Living and Working Conditions (1999): Local Community Involvement - A Handbook for Good Practices, Dublin.

Kytta, M./Horelly, L. (1997): Children's Participation in Planning and Neihborhood Improvement – a Methodological Challenge, Urban Children Conference, Norway 9–12 June 1997.

Losito B./Mayer M. (1995): Educazione ambientale: un banco di prova per l'innovazione, Rapporto Nazionale Italiano per la ricerca ENSI, CEDE, Frascati.

McKeown, R. (n.d.): Education for Sustainable Development, Toolkit, Centre for Geography and Environmental Education, University of Tennesse (www.edstoolkit.org).

Morin, E. (2000): La testa ben fatta – riforma del pensiero e riforma dell'insegnamento, Cortina, Milano.

Moro, G. (1999): Manuale di Cittadinanza Attiva, Carocci.

OECD-CERI (1994): Quality in Teaching, Parigi.

OECD-CERI (1998): Making the Curriculum Work, Parigi.

Posch, P. (1995): Professional development in environmental education: networking and infrastrucure, in Environmental Learning for the 21st century, OECD, Parigi.

Sommer, R. (1983): Social Design. Creating Buildings With People in Mind, Prentice Hall, Englewood Cliffs.

Stoltenberg, U./Nora, E. (eds., 2000): Lokale Agenda 21 – Akteure und Aktionen in Deutschland und Italien, VAS – Verlag für Akademische Schriften.

UNESCO (1997): Educating for a Sustainable Future: a Transdisciplinary Vision for Concerted Action. EDP-97/conf.401/CLD.1.

Vermeulen, W.J.V et al (1998): Planning Participation in Planning of Urban Sustainable Development: an Analysis of recent practice, URU Congress, Cities in the Treshold of the 21 Century, Utrecht.

Wynn Calder, Richard M. Clugston

U.S. Progress Toward Sustainability in Higher Education[4]

> *When society recognizes a need that can be satisfied through advanced education or research and when sufficient funds are available to pay the cost, American universities respond in exemplary fashion... On the other hand, when social needs are not clearly recognized and backed by adequate financial support, higher education has often failed to respond as effectively as it might, even to some of the most important challenges facing America ... After a major social problem has been recognized, universities will usually continue to respond weakly unless outside support is available and the subjects involved command prestige in academic circles.*
> – former Harvard University president Derek Bok (1990, p. 104-05)

Sustainable development remains barely recognized as a significant social, economic or environmental challenge for the United States. The President's Council on Sustainable Development (PCSD)[5] was disbanded in May 1999, based in part on the perception of Vice-President Albert Gore's campaign that sustainability was not an issue for the American electorate. Little funding from either governments or foundations supports higher education initiatives to promote sustain-

---

4   This chapter is a condensed version of one that originally appeared in the book *Stumbling Toward Sustainability*, John C. Dernbach ed., published by the Environmental Law Institute © 2002. All rights reserved Environmental Law Institute.
5   The PCSD was formed in June 1993 by executive order to develop policy recommendations for sustainable development in the U.S. It was a 25-member council consisting of five cabinet secretaries, chief executive officers of businesses, and executive directors of nongovernmental organizations.

able development, and only a few disciplines are beginning to afford a measure of legitimacy to teaching, research, and outreach in this area. Hopeful signs are emerging, but education for sustainable development in America is still at the margins.

The seeds of the movement to green higher education in the U.S. go back to the emergence of environmental concerns in the late 1960s and early 1970s. The first Earth Day in 1970 was a student-based effort. Internationally, the Stockholm Declaration of 1972 (United Nations 1972) related environmental concerns to all societal sectors, including education. Only after the 1992 Rio Earth Summit (United Nations 1992) did the term education for sustainable development (also "education for sustainability") enter the vocabulary of educational reformers. While the movement continues to draw on an environmental foundation, concerns have broadened to include the social and economic dimensions of sustainability.

In the U.S., higher education for sustainable development (HESD) has been given impetus over the years primarily by a small number of champions from the academy, nongovernmental organizations (NGOs) and business communities, and to a minor degree from government. In other countries (notably European, but in some developing countries as well) sustainability in higher education is supported by governments and has made deeper inroads in the disciplines and professions (Filho 1999). Some colleges and universities in the U.S. are actively pursuing an authentic commitment to sustainability, yet there is little consensus as to what the end goal looks like.

While teaching and scholarship must begin to reflect these issues, so that students learn how to think in a more integrative fashion, there is an emerging consensus that institutions must also model sustainable practices. It is important that academics keep experimenting with, and sharing, their efforts to embody sustainability, especially in making it a focus of their disciplines and professions. But it is even more critical that major stakeholders, such as the business community and funders (foundations and governments) support sustainability in higher education.

It may well be that the United States–obsessed with increasing consumption and economic growth–will not take the lead in this societal transformation. While there are increasing indications that higher education is moving toward a commitment to sustainability, there are also powerful societal forces at work against this progress. This Chapter will outline a framework for seeing sustainability reflected in the teaching and practice of higher education institutions and then report on progress since the Rio Earth Summit.

A Model Sustainable Institution

Agenda 21, various international and national HESD conferences,[6] and the numerous reports and declarations[7] they produced reflect the analysis and concerns of many constituencies in different regions of the world over the last nine years. Their understandings of the agenda for higher education to support sustainable development are remarkably similar, and they point toward a basic framework for seeing sustainability in practice. Some of these reports recognize that colleges and universities will not change without significant outside pressure–Bok's social consensus, significant (government) funding, and disciplinary prestige. Furthermore, they agree, with only few exceptions, upon a very similar ideal type of college or university, which transforms its research, teaching, outreach and operations to support sustainable development.

---

6   These include the World Conference on Higher Education (October 1998) and Yale University's Campus Earth Summit (February 1994). Since 1996 Ball State University's (Muncie, Indiana) "Greening of the Campus" conferences, held in 1996, 1997, 1999 and 2001, have promoted and helped define HESD in the U.S.
7   These include the Talloires Declaration (October 1990); the Copernicus University Charter (fall 1993); the Kyoto Declaration (November 1993); and the Thessaloniki Declaration (1997) among others.

While the manner in which academic institutions define and approach sustainability is very divergent, reflecting cultural, bioregional, economic and political diversity, we would expect a genuine commitment to creating a sustainable future to be evidenced in most of the following critical dimensions of institutional life:
- Disciplinary, professional, liberal arts and general education requirements at the university would reflect a fundamental concern for sustainability and emphasize the integrated thinking and decision making that sustainable development entails. Courses in every department (and discipline) would feature sustainability topics (e.g., Globalization and Sustainable Development; Urban Ecology and Social Justice; Population, Women and Development; Sustainable Production and Consumption; and many others). Students would also learn about how their own campus functions in the ecosystem (e.g., its sources of food, water and energy, and the endpoint of waste).
- The research of the institution would significantly focus on sustainable development (e.g., renewable energy, sustainable building design, ecological economics, population and development, environmental justice, etc.)
- Faculty and staff development and rewards at the institution would cultivate understanding of sustainable development and criteria for hiring, tenure and promotion would recognize faculty contributions to sustainability in scholarship, teaching, or campus and community activities.
- Campus operations at the college or university would be fundamentally oriented toward reducing the institution's "ecological footprint."[8] Thus one would see examples of water and energy conservation, carbon dioxide reduction practices, sustainable building

---

8   The "ecological footprint" measures human impact on nature. It indicates how much productive land and water we use to produce all the resources we consume and to take in all the waste we make. This concept, now a popular measure of sustainability, was developed by Mathis Wackernagel, who has written widely on the question of embracing limits and developing indicators to assess sustainability.

construction and renovation, environmentally responsible purchasing of food, paper and other products, etc. Furthermore, these operational practices would be integrated into the educational and scholarly activities of the school.
- Student opportunities and engagement on campus would reflect a deep commitment to sustainability through such institutional practices as new student orientation, scholarships, internships and job placement counseling related to community service, sustainability and/or justice issues. Students groups and activities focused on environmental or sustainability issues would be visibly present.
- The institution's outreach and service would support local, regional and global partnerships to enhance sustainability (e.g., collaborating with other higher education institutions, with local primary and secondary schools and with businesses to foster sustainable practices, as well as seeking international cooperation in solving global environmental justice and sustainability challenges through conferences and student/faculty exchanges).
- The university's mission, structure and planning would communicate and promote sustainability. The descriptions of learning objectives and the public relations materials of the various schools, departments, programs or offices would express prominent and explicit concern for sustainability. That commitment would be further evidenced through administrative positions and committees (e.g., Director of Environmental Programs, Sustainability Task Force, etc.) and practices (e.g., orientation programs, socially responsible investment policies, annual environmental audits, etc.).[9]

---

9   These dimensions are explored in more detail in ULSF's "Sustainability Assessment Questionnaire." See http://www.ulsf.org/programs_saq.html.

U.S. Assessment

Despite the lack of fundamental progress at the vast majority of colleges and universities, higher education in America is increasingly adopting sustainability initiatives in one or more of the seven critical dimensions of institutional life described above.[10] Innovative curricular reform for sustainability is on the rise. More research is being devoted to sustainability in the sciences, and to a lesser extent the social sciences and humanities. Some colleges and universities are modeling sustainable behavior through their purchasing, building design, and energy use. A few institutions have altered their mission statements to reflect the broader vision of a sustainable future. Particularly promising is the recent emergence of regional university partnerships and consortia, illustrating a deeper level of commitment among and between institutions, as well as recognition that such partnerships can attract funding and affect policy.

Proceeding through each dimension, we will highlight some of the best practices of pioneering institutions and assess progress.[11] In many cases, these dimensions overlap: a student's coursework may include an internship that brings her into the surrounding community to address sustainable development, thus involving the curriculum, student engagement and outreach dimensions simultaneously. To provide a clear illustration of our framework, however, we will cover each dimension separately. We will also highlight recent support for HESD from state governments and higher education associations, as well as address emerging links between the disciplines and the professions.

---

10 Both public and private institutions are implementing changes in this direction, and there is little strong evidence of differences between approaches. There are just over 4,100 accredited public and private colleges and universities in the U.S. today. A 2001 National Wildlife Federation survey shows that more than half of "campus environmental initiatives" were started within the previous five years.

11 For lack of space, we will fail to mention numerous colleges and universities engaged in important efforts in HESD. The examples referenced here are primarily illustrative.

Curriculum

At universities and colleges across the country, increasing numbers of courses that incorporate sustainability are being developed in a range of disciplines.[12] Various efforts are also underway to transform academic programs to foster interdisciplinary thinking. This is occurring despite some confusion and much debate about what sustainability means and to what extent it is relevant within the various disciplines.

Research on curriculum development at undergraduate institutions reveals several trends. It was estimated in 1995 that about 400 colleges and universities offered degrees in environmental studies or environmental science (out of approximately 3,700 higher education institutions, see O'Reilly et al. 2000). A 2001 national survey of environmental performance in higher education by the National Wildlife Federation (NWF) Campus Ecology Program indicates considerable progress with 43% of U.S. institutions surveyed offering a major or minor in environmental or sustainability studies.[13] For the most part,

---

12 Second Nature, a nonprofit organization that promotes the transformation to sustainability in higher and secondary education, supports a website with over 500 course syllabi and projects pertaining to sustainability.
See http://www.secondnature.org/resource_center/resource_center_courses.html.
See also Collett / Karakashian 1996, for thoughtful essays on incorporating sustainability into the major disciplines: Bowers 1995.

13 State of the Campus Environment, at 13. The survey also found that private colleges are four times as likely as public colleges to require most students to take a course on the environment (p.15). This was a web-based survey, distributed in three separate modules to presidents, provosts and chiefs of facilities or plant operations at over 3,900 colleges and universities. Questions covered the following topics: goals and policies, curriculum integration, environmental literacy, transportation, energy use and conservation, purchasing and recycling. There were a total of 1,116 responses from 471 presidents (or executive officers), 320 provosts (or academic officers) and 325 chief of facilities. A total of 891 institutions responded (majority public and 4-year). Data was collected from one respondent at 689 schools; two respondents at 183 schools; and all three respondents from 19 schools.
See http://www.nwf.org/campusecology/stateofthecampusenvironment/index.html.
A 2002 review of the NWF survey identifies three shortcomings: concerns about the sample's statistical significance; potential overestimation of progress; and questionable choices of indicators and metrics. See Glasser 2002, at 34–35.

however, these programs are based in biology and chemistry departments and do not teach sustainable development; nor do they make integrated thinking and decision making an integral part of their approach.

Eight percent of those schools surveyed in NWF's study actually require all students to take an environmental studies course.[14] In 1997, Oakland Community College, which serves 24,000 students in Oakland County outside of Detroit, Michigan, established a core general education requirement including one course with an in-depth focus on global environmental awareness and one course with a focus on social responsibility (Rowe n.d.). A 1995 Minnesota initiative required all state school students to take at least one "environmental theme" course.[15] Despite the relatively small number of schools requiring such courses on environmental or sustainability issues, NWF's study indicates that in 45% of universities surveyed a majority of students take at least one course concerning environmental issues.[16] Thus, while the vast majority of colleges and universities have not made sustainability a priority in the curriculum, increasing numbers are requiring or promoting this area of study in the curriculum.

Among professional schools, there are sporadic examples of education for sustainability across the spectrum, but it is too early to quantify progress in most cases. In schools of natural resources or the environment, there appears to be a trend toward explicit recognition of sus-

---

14 *Id.* at 15.
15 For more information about this requirement, see http://onestop.umn.edu/registrar/libed/index.html#THEMES.
16 State of the Campus Environment. For an assessment of U.S. institutions' progress toward "problem-focused environmental study," see Kormondy / Corcoran 1997, at 49 and 61. In this study, a 1994-95 survey of 122 universities with environmental programs (including environmental sciences, environmental studies and environmental education) revealed that the overwhelming majority of these programs were experiencing steady increases in enrollments, and that students were both following their passion for environmental protection and seeking professional and marketable skills.

tainability concerns. For example, the Yale School of Forestry & Environmental Studies "recognizes that equity and environmental progress must be combined and that a school of the environment must be a school of sustainable development."[17] Masters programs in international development, public policy and diplomacy frequently teach about sustainable development, however few programs make this integral to the coursework. Brandeis University's (Waltham, Massachusetts) Sustainable International Development Program, founded in 1994, offers an interdisciplinary Master of Arts Degree that focuses on the state of world development and issues that affect future generations. Its mission is "to help build a new generation of development planners and policy makers for whom a global society free of poverty and environmental degradation is achievable."[18] Engineering and technology schools are clearly engaging in the sustainability challenge, as the programs at Georgia Tech and other schools illustrate.

Business schools also appear to be responding to a rising interest in sustainability in the business sector. Beyond Grey Pinstripes 2001, a survey of graduate business schools in the U.S., Asia, Europe and the Americas, indicates a weak but growing commitment to teaching social and environmental issues. Fifty-eight out of approximately 403 U.S. Masters of Business Administration programs report including social and environmental topics in their courses. However, these issues are not yet being integrated into the core business curriculum and dedicated faculty remain isolated.[19] Rare exceptions include the Kenan-

---

17 See www.yale.edu/forestry/about/index.html. The University of Michigan School of Natural Resources and Environment is "dedicated to the protection of the earth's resources and the achievement of a sustainable society."
See www.snre.umich.edu/.
18 See www.heller.brandeis.edu/sid/.
19 Furthermore, the survey indicates a "disconnect" between what business leaders are requesting regarding sustainability training for MBA graduates and what business schools are in fact delivering. Beyond Grey Pinstripes 2001 is a joint project of The Aspen Institute Initiative for Social Innovation through Business and World Resources Institute. It is the third one conducted since 1998. See http://www.beyondgreypinstripes.org.

Flagler Business School at the University of North Carolina, Chapel Hill, which is well known for its dedication to "sustainable enterprises." Based on the assumption that the world will begin demanding "sustainability" within the next decade, Kenan-Flagler launched a Sustainable Enterprise Concentration Area in 1999, which provides required and recommended courses on such issues as urban reinvestment and minority economic development, environmental management systems, social marketing, life cycle management, finance and sustainability, and sustainable development.[20]

Environmental law and international environmental law are included in many law school curricula, and several law schools have programs that emphasize or provide advanced law degrees in these subjects.[21] The Widener University Law School (Harrisburg, Pennsylvania) offers a Seminar on Law and Sustainability (Dernbach et al 1997), but this kind of explicit focus on sustainability in the curriculum is rare. Notably, The George Washington University Law School established the Center on Sustainable Growth in 2000, which explores sustainable solutions to the complex problems of urban growth. The Center works closely with various departments and schools throughout the University, including the schools of Business and Public Management, Engi-

---

20 For more information on Kenan-Flagler Business School, see http://www.bschool.unc.edu/. Also of note, the Wharton School established the Zicklin Center for Business Ethics Research in 1997; and the University of Michigan Business School and the School of Natural Resources and Environment offer a joint-degree, three year Corporate Environmental Management Program. See http://www.umich.edu/~cemp/index.htm. Jonathan Lash, president of the World Resources Institute, claims that about eight business schools in the U.S. are hiring or have hired professors to teach and research in the area of sustainable enterprise.

21 See, e.g., Vermont Law School's Environmental Law Center, whose mission is "to educate for stewardship and an understanding of underlying environmental issues and values" (see http://www.vermontlaw.edu/elc/index.cfm; and New York University Center for Environmental & Land Use Law (see http://www.nyu.edu/pages/elc/index.html. Also, environmental justice courses are taught on many law school campuses. See, e.g., a description of the Thurgood Marshall School of Law Environmental Justice Clinic, available at http://www.tsulaw.edu/environ/environ.htm.

neering and Applied Science, Public Health and Health Services, and International Affairs. It hosted the first national gathering on "Smart Growth and the Law" in September 2000.[22] Other professional schools appear equally slow to consider seriously incorporating sustainability in their curricula. The deans of schools of architecture, for example, increasingly claim to be interested in sustainable design, but there is little evidence of the topic entering core areas of study. As with business schools, external interest and demand seems to exceed the readiness of architecture and design schools to seriously embrace sustainability.[23]

Research

Particularly critical to transforming American higher education is making sustainability a major research and scholarly focus. Sustainability-oriented research is increasingly funded in the sciences, but initiatives are also under way to bring the social sciences and humanities into the research dimension. The academic community has seen a rise in peer-reviewed publications focused on sustainability in higher education and on sustainability generally: the *International Journal of Sustainability in Higher Education* (Emerald) was launched in 2000; and *Environment and Sustainable Development* (Inderscience) is due in 2002. According to NWF's 2001 survey, 23% of colleges and universities support research centers that focus on "environmental" issues. The level of support for these centers, however, and the degree to which they focus on issues concerning sustainable development is unknown.

---

22 For more information on the Center on Sustainable Growth, see http://www.law.gwu.edu/csrg/default.htm.
23 Medical education has also shown little interest in embracing environmental responsibility or sustainable development. One notable effort, the Consortium for Environmental Education in Medicine (CEEM), was established by the Massachusetts Medical Society, Physicians for Social Responsibility and Second Nature in May 1994. It is now a program within Second Nature, and provides resources for teaching and incorporating environment and health perspectives into undergraduate and graduate medical education. See http://resources.secondnature.org/programs/ceem.nsf.

The Georgia Institute of Technology, along with many other engineering schools and university-based centers,[24] is helping to define the emerging field of "sustainability science." The new practitioners of sustainability science claim that in seeking "to understand the fundamental character of interactions between nature and society," the field is called upon to investigate the vast range of issues that sustainability encompasses, to do so with urgency if a crisis demands it, and to reconsider the usefulness of knowledge for both science and society. This is an action-oriented science for which a topic like climate change simultaneously demands scientific exploration and practical application. In line with Georgia Tech's research neighborhoods, this new science depends on inventive techniques and requires problem-driven, interdisciplinary research (Kates et al. 2001; National Research Council 1999).

Faculty and Staff Hiring, Development and Rewards

Few colleges and universities offer faculty development in sustainability or reward faculty for their contributions to the field. There are rare examples of schools that seek scholars with interdisciplinary training in environmental studies and another major discipline.[25] NWF's study

---

24 Such centers include the Laboratory for Sustainable Solutions (LSS) at the University of South Carolina (USC). Launched in 1997, the stated goal of LSS is to "bring awareness and understanding of industrial ecology and sustainability concepts to the forefront in South Carolina." See http://www.me.sc.edu/research/lss. Similarly, the University of Michigan's Center for Sustainable Systems (CSS), launched in 1999, develops life cycle based models and sustainability metrics for industrial systems. The Center is dedicated to interdisciplinary, multi-objective and multi-stakeholder participation. See http://css.snre.umich.edu/.

25 In 2002, the University of Vermont's School of Natural Resources sought a tenure-track scholar to specialize in the economic aspects of environmental sustainability. This faculty member is expected to develop a program of research and scholarship focused on Economics of Environmental Sustainability. Santa Clara University (Santa Clara, California) recently hired an ecological archaeologist to work half time in Environmental Studies and half-time in Anthropology, and a political ecologist to work in the Political Science and Environmental Studies departments. See Clugston/Calde, at 40.

indicates that 8% of those schools surveyed "formally evaluate or recognize how the faculty has integrated environmental topics into their courses." More surprisingly, the study shows that 50% of colleges and universities surveyed "support faculty professional development on environmental topics."[26] This finding is in keeping with the growing number of environmental studies programs in the U.S. (nearly 45% according to this study), but does not tell us the extent to which such faculty support fosters interdisciplinary work or integrated thinking in the context of sustainability. Furthermore, to the degree that scholarly attention to sustainability issues includes engagement in real world problems and public outreach (i.e., sustainability science), university departments are still far from embracing anything but "pure" research, untainted by popular writings or public speeches.[27]

Operations

While many campuses have begun to redesign their operations based on eco-efficiency, waste reduction and recycling, few schools have made a comprehensive commitment to such practices.[28] If performed well, these initiatives save money over the long-term. A 1998 report by NWF's Campus Ecology Program documented annual savings of over $15 million from 20 selected U.S. campus conservation projects

---

26 State of the Campus Environment, at 17.
27 According to one young scholar writing for *The Chronicle of Higher Education*, tenure committees "view public service as a distraction, at best irrelevant to decisions about promotion and at worst a negative sign about a faculty member's commitment to scholarship." See Sabin 2002, at B24.
28 In a 2000 study of 50 North American universities with Environmental Management Systems, Herremans and Allwright (2000) attempted to determine "What drives good performance?" The study found that those institutions most likely to be successful had high-level administrative support and long-range objectives. Herremans and Allwright conclude that "the current state of EMS at North American universities is a patchwork of independent, autonomous functions (recycling departments, facility services, plant maintenance, etc.), that are not well coordinated, nor are they working towards a common goal."

(Eagan/Keniry 1998[29]) In part for this reason, more progress has been achieved in this dimension than in any other.

As concerns about energy scarcity and prices have increased in recent years, and cost-benefit analyses look promising, efforts to conserve energy (and water) have steadily increased on campuses in the U.S. since 1992. NWF's 2001 study, for example, indicates that 81% of campuses surveyed have enacted lighting efficiency upgrades. More than half of respondents said they've developed efficiency design codes for new and old buildings, and 72% reported they have installed efficient toilets, showerheads and faucets in all or some campus units.[30] Prevalence of transportation initiatives has been disappointing, with low percentages of responding institutions reporting progress in promotion of mass transit (23% for students, 19% for employees), carpooling (17%), or minimal use of alternative fuel campus vehicles (20%).[31] A consistent finding from the NWF study is that respondents tended not to answer open-ended questions on campus energy and water consumption and waste generation. A likely reason is that respondents have neither accurate records nor regular data gathering processes.[32] This suggests a greater need for regular campus assessments so that facilities managers are both informed and encouraged to improve conservation practices.[33]

---

29 Aside from the potential financial benefits of such initiatives, a practical and moral justification stems from the fact that universities and colleges house millions of students, and the average campus generates vast amounts of waste per year, consumes millions of kilowatt hours of electricity and uses millions of gallons of water.
30 62% of campuses surveyed recycle or compost some solid waste, and 17% reported a solid waste recycling rate of 40% or more. State of the Campus Environment, at 39–40, 43.
31 *Id.* at 53.
32 *Id.* at 64–65.
33 A 2001 review of nearly 800 campus environmental assessments (in the U.S. and abroad) performed between 1989 and 2001 concluded that nearly all projects have suffered from poor intra- and inter-institutional coordination and insufficient resources, and that no accepted guidelines have been established for conducting quality assessments. This study, completed in early 2002, has made available a database of extant campus environmental assessments; an evaluation of current best practices in each assessment dimension; and a set of guidelines for performing "exemplary" assessments. See Glasser/Nixon 2001.

Student Opportunities

While student opportunities to engage in sustainability issues often arise through the university curriculum and campus outreach, this dimension is singled out to emphasize first, the centrality of students to the HESD movement, and second, the range of opportunities for students that could be further expanded in the service of sustainable development.

Numerous institutions in the U.S. have established creative programs to engage students in these issues. Harvard University's Green Campus Initiative (HGCI), for example, coordinates a summer environmental internship program, which in 2001 helped eleven student interns work directly with various administrative units within the university on practical, results-oriented projects. Project outcomes included the introduction of organic foods in the dining halls, a study on computer energy reduction, research on alternative fuel vehicles, recommendations for a sustainable buildings policy, and a greenhouse gas inventory (Powell/Sharp 2001). Also of note is the University of Colorado at Boulder's Environmental Center, which coordinates numerous activities including an award-winning recycling program. Students are directly involved in its planning and implementation in collaboration with facilities staff.[34]

Outreach and Service

There are numerous examples of innovative attempts on the part of universities and colleges to connect with their surrounding communities and beyond through projects and programs that contribute to sustainable development. Many of these involve students engaged in internships and service-learning projects, and faculty engaged in research. Service learning has increased dramatically at institutions na-

---

34 See http://www.colorado.edu/ecenter/.

tion-wide since the late 1990s. This trend has been embraced by mainstream higher education, and while it is not promoted in the name of sustainability, it is a good indication that priorities may be turning in that direction.[35]

Since 1998, state and regional partnerships and coalitions between universities, government agencies and NGO's have been forming to promote and share information on sustainability. This may represent the most significant single development in the advancement of HESD, since it indicates a growing critical mass of institutions within certain regions committed to changing state policy in support of sustainability. The New Jersey Higher Education Partnership for Sustainability (NJHEPS), for example, is a coalition of 16 New Jersey colleges and universities promoting sustainability in teaching, research, operations and outreach throughout the state.[36] The Pennsylvania Consortium for Interdisciplinary Environmental Policy, a partnership involving environmental policymakers (from the Departments of Environmental Protection and Conservation & Natural Resources) and 41 universities and colleges, is striving to overcome the traditional divide between scholarship and policy.[37]

---

[35] Service-learning actively engages students in their own educations through experiential learning in course-relevant community contexts. The American Association for Higher Education (AAHE), a major mainstream organization, started a service-learning project in the late 1990's dedicated to the integration of service-learning across the disciplines. The project has generated an 18-volume series designed to provide resources to faculty wishing to explore community-based learning through individual academic disciplines.
See http://www.aahe.org/about.htm.

[36] For more information on NJHEPS, see http://www.ramapo.edu/content/units/tas/njheps/. In a recent major achievement, NJHEPS was instrumental in getting the presidents of all New Jersey colleges and universities to sign a "Covenant of Sustainability," committing their respective institutions to a state-sponsored Sustainability Greenhouse Gas Action Plan for New Jersey (which calls for a 3.5% reduction in the state's greenhouse gas emissions by the year 2005).

[37] For more information on the Pennsylvania Consortium, see http://www.paconsortium.state.pa.us/. Current projects focus on greening the State's colleges and universities and promoting a "Sustainable Pennsylvania" by addressing climate change and energy, watershed management and land use decisions.

Institutional Mission, Structure and Planning

An institution's mission statement expresses its fundamental vision and commitment. Most university presidents and trustees are reluctant to tamper with these pronouncements, and only recently have more forward-looking schools voted to include an overt support of the environment or sustainable development. According to NWF's survey, 34% of respondents claim to have either a written declaration linking education about environmental responsibility to the school's mission, or a clear intent to do so.[38] In contrast, a 1999 study of U.S. university websites found that only 10% showed an interest in the environment in their mission statements.[39]

A less integral but significant addition to an institution's mission statement comes in the form of officially endorsed documents such as the Talloires Declaration, the only international HESD declaration that is significantly signed by U.S. university presidents. In February 1994, the total number of signatories was 179, and U.S. signatories numbered 40.[40] That number now stands at about 80.[41] This suggests a growing recognition that academic research, teaching, and service must address the sustainability challenge. However, the perennial question regarding the Talloires (and other voluntary agreements like it, including the Halifax and Copernicus declarations) is: "How many signatory schools have actually implemented the principles?" The usual answer: very few. Ball State University may be the best U.S. example

---

38 State of the Campus Environment, at 25. Many schools also have written policies on a range of environmental issues and about 25% surveyed say they plan to (28).
39 Robert Taylor (1999, at 14) conducted a content analysis of 390 randomly selected U.S. university websites. Only 7% of the websites listed or discussed environmental initiatives. The most committed universities appeared to be large, public, Northeastern schools. The survey revealed the "institutions of higher education in the United States have, for the most part, not accepted the basic principles of environmental sustainability."
40 ULSF, the Talloires Declaration secretariat, does not have accurate information prior to 1994.
41 About two-thirds of these schools are public.

of a genuine attempt to do so. After Ball State's president signed the Talloires Declaration in April 1999, the school embarked on an ambitious multi-year plan to accomplish all 10 declaration action steps. Separate committees were assigned to each step and plans of action have been drawn up with input from over 100 university representatives. The process is well underway, but significant results are yet to be seen.[42]

According to one researcher, while few signatory institutions have organized explicitly around the Talloires Declaration, many have used it as part of an overall environmental strategy, particularly to establish legitimacy for environmental efforts.[43] Three researchers studying the usefulness of international voluntary HESD declarations have criticized them for lacking compulsory requirements to demonstrate accountability. Based on a survey of 21 Talloires Declaration signatories (three from the U.S.), the researchers concluded that the Declaration was "not a crucial stimulus" to change, mostly because it lacks an implementation strategy, a monitoring process, and close guidance from the signatory secretariat (Walton/Alabaster/Jones 2000; Walton 2000).[44]

At a few universities in the U.S., staffed offices have been established with mandates to incorporate sustainability into various facets of institutional life and the surrounding community. In these rare cases, the intent of the institution is to engage in the challenge of sustainable development in a comprehensive way. Such appointments appear to be on the rise.

---

42 For a full report as of April 2001, see http://www.bsu.edu/g2.
43 This observation is based in part on a 2001 survey of U.S. Talloires Declaration signatories. See Shriberg 2002.
44 The NWF survey indicates that systems of accountability to environmental performance are present at fewer than 8% of colleges and universities. See State of the Campus Environment, at 33.

The Disciplines and Professions

It is a positive sign that numerous scholars are engaged in transforming their disciplines at both the national and local (campus) levels. Members of various professional associations have started special interest groups, divisions, or sections focused on the environment and sustainability. For example, the American Institute of Architects has a Committee on the Environment and provides an environmental education program for teachers called "Learning by Design."[45] The American Society for Engineering Education and the American Association of Engineering Societies jointly sponsor an Engineers Forum for Sustainable Development, which was founded in 1997. The American Planning Association and the American Management Association both have formed special interest groups. The American Academy of Religion has an ecology and religion section. Professional journals are emerging, such as *Ecological Economics* and the *Journal of Interdisciplinary Studies in Literature and Environment*. The latter publication provides a forum for critical studies of the literary and performing arts proceeding from or addressing environmental considerations, including ecological theory, conceptions of nature and their depictions, the human/nature dichotomy, and related concerns.[46] The May 2000 issue of *American Psychologist*, the journal of the American Psychological Association (APA), focused on "Environmental Sustainability" and its implications for the field.[47] These are at least hopeful signs of a growing movement within the disciplines and professions.

---

45 It should be noted, however, that in 1999 the National Architectural Accrediting Board significantly reduced the emphasis on sustainability in its criteria.
46 Data in this paragraph is taken largely from Clugston & Calder, at 34.
47 See Am. Psychologist, May 2000. Also, a recent issue of another APA publication features the greening of psychology (APA 2001).

Support from Government, NGOs, and Higher Education Associations

The movement to promote HESD in the U.S. has had minimal and sporadic support over the years from the federal and state governments,[48] minor but consistent support from a small number of NGOs focused on HESD, and minimal (though increasing) interest from higher education associations. Still, these various stakeholders deserve brief mention.

At the government level, environmental education is synonymous with sustainability education. The largest single source of funding and support for environmental education comes from the U.S. Environmental Protection Agency's (EPA) Office of Environmental Education (OEE). A recent government report affirms that over the past several years "Congress has appropriated less than $8 million to support OEE's programs, which in turn support programs at the international, national, state and local levels."[49] The report also affirms that funding for environmental education at the state and local levels is at best inconsistent. This situation is confirmed by a 2000 Report to Congress on the status of U.S. environmental education by the National Environmental Education Advisory Council (NEEAC), a consultative body that provides advice to the EPA on implementation of the National Environmental Education Act (1990).[50] The 2000 report states that "the overall national environmental education effort remains far weaker than it should be in terms of adequate funding, coordination and leveraging of resources, and serious evaluation and assessment tools"

---

48 State and local authorities are primarily responsible for formal education in the U.S.
49 United States of America Country Profile (December 2001). This is a superficial assessment of progress in the U.S. since Rio covering every chapter of Agenda 21. See http://citnet.org/files/USA-WSSDCountryProfileReport.pdf. This report provides brief descriptions of existing programs and projects supported primarily by the Office of Environmental Education. See www.epa.gov/enviroed.
50 NEEAC includes representatives from primary, secondary and tertiary education, state departments of education, and the business and NGO communities.

(National Environmental Education Advisory 2000, 2).[51] Furthermore, "environmental education has not been effectively infused into the educational reform movement, nor has it been institutionalized throughout K-12 or higher education. Thus, environmental education has not achieved the desired impact in government and business, or in communities" (National Environmental Education Advisory 2000, 11).

Notable exceptions to the trends in government support for environmental and sustainability related initiatives include two prominent campus greening efforts in the early 1990s and more recent initiatives in Massachusetts and Michigan. EPA gave initial funding to Tufts University and The George Washington University (GW) in 1990 and 1994 respectively. These initiatives met with varying success, and support for the GW initiative was short-lived due to changing priorities at EPA.[52] In 2000, EPA and the Massachusetts Executive Office of Environmental Affairs (EOEA) provided $65,000 to conduct an assessment of the four (non-medical school) University of Massachusetts campuses to ascertain the level of education for sustainability activities and to develop plans to foster such programs. The EOEA refunded this project in 2001 to further the implementation of sustainability programs.[53] Also in 2000, EPA awarded Michigan State University (one of the largest single campuses in the U.S.) $250 thousand dollars to develop a campus sustainability program.[54]

---

51 www.epa.gov/enviroed.
52 For information on the George Washington University's "Green University Initiative," see www.gwu.edu/~greenu/. For information on "Tufts CLEAN!," see Creighton (1998), 1-3.
53 To date, the chancellors at every campus have been persuaded to appoint and charge official campus sustainability committees. Walter Bickford is directing the project out of the University of Massachusetts, Boston Urban Harbors Institute. See http://www.uhi.umb.edu/.
54 See www.msu.edu/unit/vprgs/RN%20Summer%202000/EPA%20grant.htm.

States are supporting HESD efforts in small but significant ways: South Carolina contributed to the Sustainable Universities Initiative in 2000; Pennsylvania gives basic support to the Pennsylvania Consortium; and New Jersey has contributed seed money to the Partnership for Sustainability there (see "Outreach and Service" section above). The Minnesota Office of Environmental Assistance (MOEA) has recently funded several projects in higher education: campus greening conferences in 2000 and 2001; an ongoing ecological footprint project of the University of Minnesota (UM) Sustainable Campus Initiative and a UM Center for Sustainable Building Research.

Since the early 1990's, four U.S. NGOs committed to promoting sustainability in higher education have helped articulate both the nature of a sustainable university and strategies for moving forward. These are the National Wildlife Federation's Campus Ecology Program,[55] Second Nature,[56] University Leaders for a Sustainable Future (ULSF),[57] and World Resources Institute's Sustainable Enterprise Program.[58] In 1996, these NGOs formed an Alliance for Sustainability through Higher Education to be a stronger voice for university reform. The

---

[55] The Campus Ecology Program assists students, faculty, staff and administrators with the design and implementation of practical conservation projects, providing training and incentives, and helping to document and share lessons learned. It has recently published the higher education survey used extensively in this chapter. See http://www.nwf/campus.

[56] Second Nature supported networking among stakeholder groups and faculty/staff development through interactive workshops and disseminated 'best practices' resources. See http://www.secondnature.org.

[57] ULSF is the secretariat for signatories of the Talloires Declaration, publishes case studies, provides sustainability assessment and evaluation, conducts research on HESD in the U.S. and promotes international partnerships and projects to support HESD abroad. See http://www.ulsf.org. Second Nature ceased its operations in May 2002. The website still exists but no longer supports a large database of resources.

[58] Formerly the Management Institute for Environment and Business, WRI's Sustainable Enterprise Program works to infuse environmental principles throughout the core disciplines at business schools across the U.S. and in Latin America. WRI also sponsors the business school survey cited in the *Curriculum* sub-section above. See http://www.wri.org/wri/meb/.

Alliance played a significant role in ensuring that higher education was included in the program of the National Town Meeting for a Sustainable America in May 1999, an unprecedented gathering of over 3,000 Americans aimed to inspire a national movement toward sustainability. Following the National Town Meeting, which was co-sponsored by the President's Council on Sustainable Development, the PCSD disbanded (as anticipated), and the energy generated there quickly dissipated.[59] The lesson learned was that sustainability was still not a national priority. These NGOs continue, however, to promote the HESD agenda by providing information and assistance, and working with institutions and individuals committed to slow but steady transformation. In January 2000, they helped launch a Higher Education Network for Sustainability and the Environment (HENSE), which expanded the original Alliance to provide a more powerful platform for faculty, students and professionals in the U.S. and Canada to share information, collaborate on HESD projects and more rapidly advance the movement.[60]

Recent efforts of the National Council for Science and the Environment (NCSE) are very encouraging.[61] Due largely to NCSE's work, the National Science Board in February 2000 approved a report, Environmental Science and Engineering for the 21st Century: the role of the National Science Foundation, which recommended that NSF funding for environmental research, education, and scientific assessment should be increased by $1 billion over the next five years, to reach an annual expenditure of approximately $1.6 billion. This could be critical as an external stimulus for university research on sustainability

---

59 The National Town Meeting was also sponsored by the Global Environment and Technology Foundation. See http://www.sustainableusa.org/ntm/.
60 HENSE has supported various HESD projects and continues as an informal network, raising money as needed. Go to the Resources Database at www.ulsf.org for more information on HENSE.
61 NCSE (formerly the Committee for the National Institute for the Environment) is a non-profit organization, working since 1990 to improve the scientific basis for environmental decision making and supported by nearly 500 academic, scientific, environmental, and business organizations. See http://cnie.org/NCSE.

related issues. NCSE has attracted leaders from the academic, scientific, governmental, environmental and business sectors to its annual National Conference on Science, Policy, and the Environment. Sustainability science and its application has been a central theme of the first two conferences held in 2000 and 2001, and breakout groups have discussed the role of higher education in sustainability. The third NCSE conference, to be held in January 2003 will have as its theme "Education for a Sustainable and Secure Future." NCSE has also recently established a Council of Environmental Deans and Directors (CEDD), which include the deans of colleges of environment and natural resources and directors of institutes of environmental studies at more than 40 universities and colleges. The new organization facilitates peer-to-peer communication and collaboration and external relations with federal agencies, the U.S. Congress, employers and NGOs. This network will be a powerful force for engaging internal and external stakeholders in the pursuit of sustainability in higher education.

Some higher education associations, like their disciplinary counterparts, are beginning to pay attention to sustainability issues. The Society for College and University Planning (SCUP), the Association of Physical Plant Administrators of Universities and Colleges (APPA) and APPA's strategic partner, the Professional Grounds Maintenance Society (PGMS), have identified environmental issues as an important global concern that must be addressed by the organizations' constituencies through specific initiatives. The American Association for Higher Education (AAHE) and the Association of Governing Boards of Universities and Colleges (AGB) are also starting to look seriously at the challenge of sustainability for higher education and recognize the need to educate their constituencies on the issues involved.[62]

---

62 AGB managed to get "sustainability" on the short list of priorities for governing boards in 1999 and 2000. However, other concerns took precedence in 2001. AGB also devoted the entire spring 2000 issue of its membership publication, "Priorities," to HESD (see Clark 2000, at 1-16). The general data on higher education associations is taken from Morri 2000.

Clearly, most of the motivation and funding for HESD in the U.S. are coming from within. This is occurring despite tremendous barriers to change within the structures of higher education. In all of the major dimensions of higher education identified in this section, there is evidence of reform for sustainability on campuses across the U.S. The numerous projects, programs and initiatives that have been discussed here indicate a significant effort on the part of many individual faculty, administrators, students and staff to change the institutions in which they work to better reflect our fundamental challenges in the world at large.

Conclusion

The United States has barely acknowledged Agenda 21, let alone attempted to implement it. But despite our failure to address the worsening environmental, social and economic trends here and around the world, we are making progress in understanding how to create a sustainable future. The theoretical framework and practical models are being clarified; the knowledge, skills, and sensibilities are emerging. The direction we need to go is becoming clearer: We must change the economic bottom line to value full human development in healthy ecosystems; we must eliminate subsidies for unsustainable practices; and we must shift production and consumption patterns to eliminate violence and poverty, to support all life, future generations, and social justice. We must also recognize our limits and honor the deeper meaning and mystery of life (Clugston, R.M. 2002).[63]

---

63 The Earth Charter, an international declaration of fundamental principles for building a just, sustainable and peaceful global society in the 21st century, has emerged today as one of the most elegant and comprehensive definitions of sustainability. Completed in March 2000, the Earth Charter is part of the unfinished business of the Rio Earth Summit. It is increasingly being seen as a tool for sustainability education and an international Earth Charter education program has been launched.

Many academic institutions have focused on greening their campus operations. Some have transformed their curricula to reflect the complexities and values of sustainable development. A few have positioned themselves as leading "sustainable universities." Yet, when a critical champion leaves, when major external funding dries up, or when staff seek to move from rhetoric to reality, these initiatives often reveal their lack of real support in the institution. Thus, sustainability initiatives meet with various degrees of success. In some institutions, seemingly broad-based and strong initiatives have faded away. In others, significant academic programs and operations policies have been institutionalized. Despite the many impressive initiatives in progress around the U.S., the deeper challenge of transforming the disciplines to teach integrated thinking for sustainability–and placing value on this transformation–eludes us.

American higher education can be very innovative and adaptive. Leaders in a variety of institutions have grasped the critical need for sustainable development, and they have created a variety of exemplary responses. However these innovations will never move into the mainstream until critical stakeholders demand it. Al Gore, in *Earth in the Balance*, said that the environment must become a central organizing principle for the 21st Century (Gore 1999). He went on to propose a massive federal initiative–like the Marshall Plan–to fund the transition to a sustainable future. The same Al Gore, as a presidential candidate eight years later, closed down the PCSD, in part because he did not think sustainability would get him elected. Gore was right the first time and perhaps the second time too. Educators need to raise public concern, lobby for funding, and work within the disciplines to make real progress toward higher education for sustainable development in the U.S. But success, as Bok points out, will depend ultimately on the demands that the disciplines, professions, and funders place on higher education.

References

APA (2001): Monitor on Psychology, Apr. 2001.
Bok, D. (1990): Universities and the Future of America.
Bowers, C.A. (1995): Educating for an Ecologically Sustainable Future.
Clark, C.S. (2000): Campuses Move Toward Sustainability, Priorities. Ass'n of Governing Boards, Spring 2000.
Clugston, R.M. (2002): Towards the World Summit on Sustainable Development, Earth Ethics, CRLE spring 2002.
Clugston, R.M./Calder, W. (n.d.): Critical Dimensions of Sustainability in Higher Education, in: Sustainability and University Life.
Collett, J./Karakashian, S. (eds., 1996): Greening the College Curriculum.
Dernbach, J. and the Widener University Law School Seminar on Law and Sustainability (1997): U.S. Adherence to its Agenda 21 Commitments: A Five-Year Review, 27 ELR 10504 (Oct. 1997).
Eagan, D.J./Keniry, J. (1998): National Wildlife Federation's Campus Ecology Progam, Green Investment, Green Return: How Practical Conservation Projects Save Millions on America's Campuses.
Filho, W. L. (1999): Sustainability and University Life: Some European Perspectives, in: W.L. Filho (ed.), Sustainability and University Life, vol. 5.
Glasser, H. (2002): Murky Grades on Campus Sustainability, Trusteeship, The Association of Governing Boards of Universities and Colleges, March/April 2002.
Glasser, H./Nixon, A. (2001): Western Michigan University, A Comprehensive Review of Campus Sustainability Assessments.
Gore, A. (1993): Earth in the Balance: Ecology and the Human Spirit. Reprint.
Herremans, I./Allwright, D.E. (2000): Environmental Management systems at North American Universities: What Drives Good Performance?, 1 Int'l J. of Sustainability in Higher Education, 168.
Kates, R.W. et al. (2001), Sustainability Science, 292 Sci. 641 (Apr. 27, 2001).

Kormondy, E.J./Corcoran, P.B. (1997): Environmental Education: Academia's Response. North American Ass'n for Envtl. Education.

Morri, A. (2000): Working with Higher Education Organizations for a More Sustainable Future. NWF Campus Ecology Program 2000.

National Environmental Education Advisory (2000): Council Report to Congress II, September 28, 2000.

National Research Council (1999): Our Common Journey: A Transition Toward Sustainability.

O'Reilly, D. et al. (2000): Environmental Studies.

Powell, A./Sharp, L. (2001): Environmental Internships Changing Harvard University, The Declaration (Dec. 2001).

Rowe, D. (n.d.): Environmental Literacy and Sustainability as Core Degree Requirements: Success Stories and Models, in Greening of the Campus IV (abstract).

Sabin, P. (2002): Academe Subverts Young Scholars' Civic Orientation, Chron. Higher Educ., Feb. 8, 2002.

Shriberg, M. (2002): Sustainability Leadership in Higher Education: Motivations, Methods and Outcomes Among Leading U.S. 4-year Institutions (working title), doctoral dissertation, University of Michigan, School of Natural Resources & Environment, forthcoming 2002.

Taylor, R.W. (1999): Environmental Sustainability in Higher Education: A Survey Analysis, The Declaration (Sept. 1999).

United Nations (1972): Declaration of the United Nations Conference on the Human Environment, June 16, 1972.

United Nations (1992): Declaration on Environment and Development of the United Nations Conference on Environment and Development, June 14, 1992.

Walton, J. (2000): Should Monitoring Be Compulsory within Voluntary Environmental Agreements, 8 Sustainable Dev., 146 (2000).

Walton, J./Alabaster, T./Jones, K. (2000): Environmental Accountability: Who's Kidding Whom?, 26 Envtl. Mgmt., 525 (2000).

IV.
Ways to Institutionalize the Concepts

Peter Blaze Corcoran and Emanuel Rogier van Mansvelt

On the Meaning of Institutional Commitment and Institutional Assessment

Introduction

> *The ultimate goal of education for sustainable development is to impart the knowledge, values, attitudes and skills needed to empower people to bring about the changes required to achieve sustainability.*
> Lüneburg Declaration 2001

What if the signing of the COPERNICUS-Charter by your university did not bring about such changes? What if the signing of the COPERNICUS-Charter by all 281 signatories did not bring about such changes? What if the commitments to the Talloires Declaration, the Halifax Declaration, the Swansea Declaration, the Kyoto Declaration, and the COPERNICUS-Charter by over a thousand universities throughout the world did not lead to the goal of education for sustainable development? How would we know? How *can* we know what such commitments mean? How can we know if they are earnest and principled? How can we evaluate institutional change and the institutional capacity to impart the knowledge, values, attitudes, and skills upon which the premise of the Lüneburg Declaration rests?

This essay is based on the assumption that as we move toward education for sustainable development in higher education, the institutional commitments in place and the institutional assessments underway must have meaning and integrity. In this essay, we elaborate on the meaning of higher education for sustainable development and the need for institutional commitment and institutional assessment.

We need new challenges, new visions, and new methods in order to change universities. We have to deepen the meaning of sustainable development by redefining the purpose of teaching and scientific research. We must reorient institutional commitment toward sustainable development. And we need new assessment tools to measure if we really are making such changes.

Many universities have signed a charter on sustainable development because they agreed in some way or the other with the Brundtland definition of sustainable development- development that "meets the needs of the present without compromising the ability of future generations to meet their own needs" (World Commission on Environment and Development 1987). At the same time the practical meaning of sustainable development is unclear. What does it mean for a university? What are the consequences of adopting a vision on sustainable development? What are the problems to overcome? What results can be identified? What are the benefits for students, staff, teachers, and researchers?

In ten years, the term sustainable development has become widespread and used in thousands of books, reports, and policies. The developed world is keen on using the first part, "sustainable"; while the developing countries focus rather on the second part, "development". In Western society an interesting phenomenon is occurring—"sustainable" or "sustainability" appear to be more and more fashionable and trendy words. Commercials talk about "sustainable cars" and "sustainable haircolour" and the Dutch Railway offers a discount if you have a "sustainable relationship"—longer than one year! Sustainability is a synonym for things that will last for a long time. By using just the term sustainable or sustainability the full concept of sustainable development is lost. We believe the strength of sustainable development is in the meaning of the two words combined.

Sustainable development opens a new realm of possibilities for universities. All university activities have something to do with the opportunity to make the world a better place. Present professors teach future entrepreneurs, philosophers, and politicians. Present scientists explore the universe for new universal knowledge and understanding. Currently the focus of teaching and research is narrow and discipline-oriented. Students learn to think extremely well in their field of study but they often know little of other disciplines and are not able to act upon their knowledge in a universal way. Sustainable development provides an important opportunity for institutions of higher education to unite their activities in a flow toward sustainable development. Universities can contribute in a sustainable way to the development of all fields. The result can be a magnificent renaissance of the meaning of university.

Since the 1992 United Nations Conference on Environment and Development in Rio, many universities have agreed on the importance of sustainable development by signing a declaration of commitment to sustainable development. Progress has been made, but only a very few institutions have managed to redefine mission, redesign education, reorient research, and significantly improve campus-management.

Institutional Commitment – Possibilities and Problems

Titular agreement with declarations has enormous potential for advancing the movement toward higher education for sustainable development. The role of top administrative leadership in advancing institutional change is widely understood. It is not always sufficient to make change, but it is almost always necessary. If the university leader sets a tone of engagement for advancing education for sustainable development, it can give rise to new programs and can strengthen current initiatives of students and faculty. Leaders can support scholarly activity and faculty rewards—traditionally those areas in which change is most intractable.

Hans van Ginkel, Rector of the United Nations University in Tokyo, Japan, was among the first university leaders in Europe to put sustainable development on the university agenda. His efforts provide an inspiring example of commitment by a university leader. Even before 1992, the year of the Rio de Janeiro conference on sustainable development, Van Ginkel participated in a network between Western and Eastern Europe, at that time divided by the iron curtain. In 1993 as a rector of the University of Utrecht in the Netherlands, Van Ginkel initiated and signed the COPERNICUS-Charter (Filho 1996).

Endorsement by university leaders is of critical importance in moving universities toward sustainable development. The moral responsibility of institutions to participate in the movement of society toward sustainability is of critical importance in building momentum to make the changes called for by the Lüneburg Declaration. Knowing that the issue is taken seriously elsewhere, gives it seriousness.

Schools in many parts of the world compete for the best students. Since social justice and care for the environment are concerns of the young, the best and most committed students will seek programs and universities that can address their concerns. This can build momentum for other schools to follow.

A Dutch example of student leadership shows how much can be accomplished[64]. In 1995, students in the Netherlands started to move universities to integrate sustainable development in all aspects of university life. In 1998 a network was founded by motivated students and teachers from different universities and people engaged in higher education from ministries to NGO's. They started working without funding and without an official organisation. Now, after six years a flourishing network is expecting major results in the coming years. The project groups design tools for education for sustainable development.

---

64 See for more on this: The Dutch success story, higher education for sustainable development, chapter XXX of this book.

The network coordinates projects on interdisciplinary education nationally and internationally, challenging experts for sustainable development in different disciplines, exploring strategies for innovation and assessment in curricula.[65]

Universities sign charters with a variety of motivations. It might be a positive sign to the outside world, an act of compassion concerning the future of the world, a belief that the university can contribute to solving problems related to sustainable development, or a vision that the university could play a major leading role in all fields of sustainable development.

The worst case, we suppose would be signing a declaration as a way of demonstrating a commitment that did not exist. We know of no such cynical act of "green washing" and hope not to know them in the future. Yet clearly, some institutional commitments are more principled and sincere than others and some commitments are made with much more understanding than others of how difficult a task it is to keep them.

Much more common, we believe, is making a well-intentioned commitment with no institutional plan and no allocation of resources to realize it. Resistance to change in higher education is legendary. Many factors, ranging from lack of financial resources, to the complexity of universities, to faculty loyalty to traditional disciplines, make new ideas difficult to implement. Even the most earnest commitments can go unrealised.

---

65 see footnote 64

Institutional Assessment – Possibilities and Problems

Each university is a small universe in itself. It is a huge and complex institution. The university is as a part of society in general (Van Weenen 1999). During the last ten years more and more universities have initiated projects relating to sustainable development. Some of them came to a certain point where they needed to know if they were developing in a sustainable direction. Were they really contributing to sustainable development? We believe that to take sustainable development seriously, it must be evaluated.

The complexity of the organisation becomes clear when evaluating a university concerning sustainable development. Evaluation can be accomplished with many different kinds of tools. These tools vary from structures for implementation, visions for management, and charters, to audit instruments, good practices, and certification. The challenge for universities is to develop an integrated vision for sustainable development including projects, plans and policies for the operational management, education and research.

For the operational management there is a set of very good tools. The best and most comprehensive are International Standard Organisation (ISO) 14001 and Environmental Management System (EMAS 1993) certification. In Sweden and Germany some universities are ISO 14001 ore EMAS certified.

Many universities have an effective operational management system. But the system is often based on the guidelines and restrictions of the national laws and environmental rules. Many institutions do not have adequate control of operational management because they hire companies outside the university itself. Even if a university has hired companies for operational management it can include negotiations about environmental aspects. Students can be involved to evaluate the operational management and do so as part of their study.

Education is the core business of a university. Students will be the teachers and researchers of tomorrow. They will be managers, politicians, and take key positions in future's society. How will they learn responsibility, values, and to care for future generations?

Sustainable development opens tremendous opportunities to redesign education. If a university takes a stand for sustainable development all teachers can accept the challenge to redesign their education. A successful, proven strategy to involve teachers from all kinds of disciplines is to challenge them for sustainable development (Dankelman, 2002). In the Netherlands teachers from all kinds of disciplines are invited to write a book about the possibilities and challenges for their own discipline to contribute to sustainable development. Many teachers took the opportunity to do research and write recommendations to integrate sustainable development in curricula.

Regular quality assessment systems on education are perhaps the most effective way for faculties to redesign curricula. By taking sustainable development as a leading principle in these assessments, faculties are motivated to integrate sustainable development in curricula (VSNU 2000). Today, many countries are designing new models and strategies for accreditation. We encourage those involved in accreditation to make sustainable development one of the guidelines or leading principles.

Perhaps the most comprehensive assessment instrument developed is the Auditing Instrument for Sustainable development in Higher Education (AISHE), an initiative by the Dutch national network for Higher Education for Sustainable Development. The AISHE instrument is developed to evaluate education. It is a comprehensive instrument assessing how sustainable development is integrated in the vision and policy, management, communication, staff development, research, environmental management, education and evaluation of a curricula. The instrument has two main objectives. The first is to find out how sustainable development is integrated in a certain curricula. The second is to give concrete ideas to improve education for sustainable development. This year, in the Netherlands fifteen universities will use AISHE (Roorda 2002) to improve the quality of curricula using sustainable development as a leading principle.

University Leaders for a Sustainable Future in Washington, D.C. has identified seven critical dimensions of university life on which sustainable development can be assessed. They are curriculum, research and scholarship operations, community outreach and service, student opportunities, institutional mission and structure and faculty and staff development and rewards. All these offer exciting possibilities for making sustainability central to university life.

One major issue for engaged teachers and entrepreneurs, willing to change higher education for sustainable development, is freedom of education. A common feeling is that education should be free of values and guidelines. Many government departments on education do not want to tell universities what to teach. Even university boards have nothing to say concerning the content of education. This freedom of education is a precious value to maintain. The only way sustainable development works is if the students and teachers are motivated to contribute. Often teachers would like to address sustainable development but do not have the time to even think about it. Administrative leadership should take these complains serious and allocate resources for teachers who want to change education. University boards need to create an environment for students, teachers, researchers and staff to adopt sustainable development—and evaluate their success.

The field of research and sustainable development is enormous. In the first place there are research areas directly connected to sustainable development such as the greenhouse effect, depletion of the ozone layer, chemical pollution, and environmental management. In these research fields millions of dollars are spent to assess consequences for human beings now and in the future. The second field, less explored, is about the social, cultural, and economic dimensions of sustainable development. We must ask if research is contributing to sustainable development in one-way or the other.

A major opportunity is to bring sustainable development as a vision for research in this arena. Sustainable development does not produce laws or rules but opens a realm for discussion. Universities and governmental funders could ask researchers to speak to sustainable development in their research proposals.

Beside regular and serious assessment of physical operations, education, and research on sustainable development, university and faculty leaders need to professionalize their effort and policies for implementation. A major problem with the assessment of progress toward sustainability is that commitments are made without the establishment of standards, protocols, or, even, evaluation strategies. Baseline data are not gathered later, weakening even accomplishments that seem significant.

As with much educational research, the application of an established methodology to a new field of endeavour can be challenging in its early stages. For example, case study methodology in higher education for sustainable development is inchoate and underdeveloped. Most case studies are, in effect, case stories or make-your case studies in which important insights are shared but which lack strong theoretical or methodological rigor (Corcoran 2002).

In any sense, this is difficult research—the efforts of environmental education research to measure "the knowledge, values, attitudes, and skills" referred to in the Lüneburg Declaration have long been problematic. Nevertheless, researcher integrity calls upon us to utilize and advance existing instruments and approaches to assess the complex constellation of factors that education for sustainable development impacts in empowering students to spur change. Clearly, the challenge for assessment is to develop methods to capture the complexity of the institutions and the institutional change involved.

Universities are enormously complex—a university is like a hundred businesses and is as complex in many ways as is society. Sustainable development is a multidimensional and difficult-to-define concept. It can conceivably affect every dimension of university life. Recent research initiatives like the University Leaders for a Sustainable Future Sustainability Assessment Questionnaire and the AISHE model seek to address this complexity systematically. Problems of assessment can be reduced by having a strategy for each aspect of higher education - and a clear definition of the contextual meaning of sustainability as part of that strategy.

While we acknowledge the contestation and problematic surrounding the meaning of sustainable development, and the challenges to the researcher in assessing sustainable development, we believe it must not only be preached but evaluated too. We support efforts to create assessment methodologies that are philosophically consistent with the aims of the institution's sustainable development initiative.

Evaluation procedures must have meaning for the institution and validity for others. Institutional assessments ought to have accountability to both the research community and to the wider community of stakeholders in higher education. These include students, faculty, trustees, and administrators themselves.

Final Remarks and Conclusion

In 2000, four organizations agreed to form a Global Higher Education for Sustainability Partnership (GHESP), to combine their strengths in an effort to mobilize higher education institutions to support sustainable development. The organizations are:
- The Association of University Leaders for a Sustainable Future (ULSF) serves as the Secretariat of over 280 signatories of the Talloires Declaration in over 40 countries and promotes education for sustainability based on the Earth Charter;

- COPERNICUS-Campus, formerly a Programme of the Association of European Universities, is responsible for the University Charter for Sustainable Development, signed to date by over 290 university leaders in 36 European countries;
- The International Association of Universities (IAU) provides an international centre of cooperation among 800 member universities and institutions of higher education. IAU developed and adopted the Kyoto Declaration;
- The United Nations Educational, Scientific, and Cultural Organization (UNESCO) is the task manager for the implementation of Chapter 36, "Education, Public Awareness and Training" of *Agenda 21* and for the international work programme on education of the United Nations Commission on Sustainable Development.

GHESP partners believe that higher education must play a central role within the overall process of achieving sustainable development. The partners are convinced that if the leaders of major disciplines and institutions do not make sustainable development a central academic and organizational focus, it will be impossible to create a just, equitable, and sustainable future.

Together IAU, ULSF and COPERNICUS represent over 1000 universities that have committed to making sustainable development a central focus of their teaching and practice. Roughly one third of these signatory institutions are from the global South, and one-fifth from countries in the former Soviet Union and Warsaw Pact nations. Such diversity and numbers of institutions can advance the possibilities of institutional commitment through sharing of ideas and strategies and through common endeavours.

The Talloires and Kyoto Declarations, the University Charter of COPERNICUS and other international statements like them, have contributed to a global consensus on higher education for sustainable development. The themes which nearly all international declarations share include promoting sustainable development in all relevant disciplines, research on sustainable development issues, the 'greening' of university operations, engaging in inter-university cooperation, forming partnerships with government, NGOs and industry, and most consistently, the moral obligation of higher education to work for a sustainable future.

We believe such Declarations and such partnerships as GHESP with its Lüneburg declaration can help define the meaning of institutional commitment and institutional assessment. We hope, as we move toward the World Summit on Sustainable Development in Johannesburg and beyond, to see renewed commitment tied to institutional action and evaluation plans- and to see many strategic partnerships among institutions committed to education for sustainable development.

References

Calder, W./Clugston, R.M. (2002): Progress towards sustainability in higher education. In: Dernbach (ed.), Sustainable Development in the United States Ten Years After the Earth Summit. Washington DC. In press.

COPERNICUS-Campus, Lüneburg Declaration, www.copernicus-campus.org.

Corcoran, P.B./Wals, E.E.J./Walker (2002): Case studies, case stories, and make-your-case studies: a critique of case study methodology. A paper presented at American Educational Research Association.

Dankelen, I./Vlasman, A. (in progress). Nulde review over Hoger Onderwijs en Duurzame ontwikkeling.

Environmental Management System (EMAS) (1993): European Commission, Council Regulations 1836/93.

Filho, W.L./MacDermott, F./Padgham, J. (1996): Implementing sustainable development at university life. A Manual of good practice. CRE-Copernicus. University of Bradfort, Bradford.

Filho, W.L. (1999): Sustainability and university life. Frankfurt am Main, Peter Lang Publishers.
International Organization for Standardization (ISO), http://www.iso.ch/
Kormondy, E./Corcoran, P.B. (1997): Environmental Education: Academia's Response. Troy, OH: North American Association for Environmental Education.
Roorda, N. (2001): Auditing Instrument for Sustainability in Higher Education (AISHE). University of Amsterdam, Amsterdam.
University Leaders for a Sustainable Future (1999): Sustainability Assessment Questionaire (SAQ).
Van Weenen (1999): Towards a vision of a sustainable university. In: Filho, W.L., International Journal of Sustainability in Higher Education. 2000. MCB University Press. Hamburg.
VSNU (2000): Scheikunde en Scheikundige Technology. VSNU. Utrecht.
Wals, E.E.J./Jickling, B. (2002): Process-based Environmental Education: Setting Standards without Standardizing. In: Jensen, B.B./Schnack, K./Simovska, V. (eds.), Critical Environmental and Health Education. Copenhagen: Royal School of Education Studies.
World Commission on Environment and Development (1987): Our Common Future. Oxford University Press: Oxford.

Peter Blaze Corcoran

The Earth Charter: An Ethical Framework for "Good" Globalization

A premise of the Lüneburg Declaration is that higher education for sustainable human development is a critical component of efforts to humanize globalization. Worldwide exchange of capital, products, and a culture of consumption are with us; but if globalization is to mean more than transnational corporate commidification of resources and cultural concepts, it needs an ethical framework.

Steven C. Rockefeller, Chair of the Drafting Committee of the Earth Charter, has said:

> We urgently need a shared vision of basic values that will provide a basis for world wide partnership and an ethical foundation for the emerging world community. The mission of the Earth Charter initiative is to help establish such a foundation. The Earth Charter endeavors to make clear that in the final analysis the problems the world faces are ethical ones. Rockefeller 2001, p. 7

If the problems we face are, in the end, ethical problems, then, indeed, the solutions must be solutions to which ethics point. We need an ethical framework for sustainability in the context of globalization. In this brief essay, I will argue that the Earth Charter, by virtue of its remarkable birthright and content can provide a higher education with such a foundation for humane and just globalization.

Another premise of the Lüneburg Declaration is that education in all its forms plays an indispensable role in addressing the crucial challenges of sustainable development. Higher education, with its powerful concentration of intellectual resources and privileged position in society, has a leadership role, indeed, a moral responsibility, to seek ethical and practical answers to the economic, social, and environmental problems caused by globalization. Higher education, then, can take the lead in pointing the way toward an integrated vision of the challenges and the solutions. I believe that the Earth Charter, recognizing as it does the indivisibility of environmental protection, human rights, equitable human development, and peace, is a wholesome conception of sustainability that can assist higher education in its response to globalization.

History and Structure of the Earth Charter[66]

> *We must join together to bring forth a sustainable global society founded on respect for nature, universal human rights, economic justice, and a culture of peace. Towards this end, it is imperative that we, the peoples of earth, declare our responsibility to one another, to the greater community of life, and to future generations.* Earth Charter Commission 2000, Preamble

The drafting of an Earth Charter was part of the unfinished business of the 1992 Rio Earth Summit. In 1994, Maurice Strong, Secretary General of the Earth Summit and Chairman of the Earth Council, and Mikhail Gorbachev, the President of Green Cross International, launched a new Earth Charter initiative in The Hague with support from the Dutch government. An Earth Charter Commission was formed in 1997 to oversee the project, and an Earth Charter Secretariat was established at the Earth Council in Costa Rica.

To the best of our knowledge, the Earth Charter Initiative has involved the most open and participatory consultation process ever conducted in connection with the drafting of an international document. Tens of thousands of individuals and hundreds of organizations from all regions of the world, different cultures and diverse sectors of society

---

[66] This section relies on several descriptions of the process and content of the Earth Charter and especially the Earth Charter Briefing Book (Earth Charter International Secretariat 2000) and The Earth Charter Initiative Handbook (Earth Charter International Secretariat 2001).

have participated. The Charter has been shaped by experts, government and civil society leaders, students, and representatives from indigenous groups and grassroots communities. I believe it is an important expression of the hopes and aspirations of the emerging global society. It is part of a growing worldwide people's movement pursuing major challenges in our values and institutions in order to ensure a better future for all. It is, truly, a people's charter.

A final version of the document was released by the Earth Charter Commission in March 2000, and a new phase of the Earth Charter Initiative began, which involved circulation of the document as a people's treaty throughout the world in an effort to promote awareness and commitment to a sustainable way of life. The major objectives of the Earth Charter Initiative are to promote a worldwide dialogue on shared values and global ethics; to set forth a succinct and inspiring vision of fundamental ethical principles for sustainable development; circulate the Earth Charter throughout the world as a people's treaty, promoting awareness, commitment, and implementation of Earth Charter values; and seek endorsement of the Earth Charter by the United Nations General Assembly.

The Preamble of the Earth Charter briefly describes the cosmological and ecological situation and the major challenges and choices facing humanity. There follow sixteen main principles, which are divided into four parts. Each part contains four main principles with a number of supporting principles that elaborate the meaning of the main principles. The principles in the Charter are formulations of fundamental ethical guidelines and major strategies. The Charter does not attempt to describe the mechanisms and instruments required to implement its principles. This is a task for other international legal instruments and for national and local sustainable development plans.

A Pedagogy for Globalization

As never before in history, common destiny beckons us to seek a new beginning. Such renewal is the promise of these Earth Charter principles. To fulfill this promise, we must commit ourselves to adopt and promote the values and objectives of the Earth Charter.

> This requires a change of mind and heart. It requires a new sense of global interdependence and universal responsibility. We must imaginatively develop and apply the vision of a sustainable way of life locally, nationally, regionally, and globally. Our cultural diversity is a precious heritage and different cultures will find their own distinctive ways to realize the vision. We must deepen and expand the global dialogue that generated the Earth Charter, for we have much to learn from the ongoing collaborative search for truth and wisdom. Earth Charter Commission 2000, "The Way Forward"

Such advancement of high-minded values, such changes of mind and heart, and such senses of interdependence and responsibility across culture can only be achieved through education. Realizing culturally-rooted visions of sustainability and searching for cross-cultural collaboration is, inherently, a process of education. The Earth Charter Initiative has said from the beginning that the Earth Charter is an educational resource of significant value. According to the Earth Charter Briefing Book,

> *Discussion of the Earth Charter in classrooms, conferences, and workshops can heighten awareness of the basic challenges and choices that face humanity. It can help people learn to think globally and holistically. It can focus attention on fundamental ethical issues and their interconnectedness. It can serve as a catalyst for cross-cultural and interfaith dialogue on shared values and global ethics. It can be used to generate in individuals and communities the kind of internal reflection that leads to a change in attitudes, values, and behavior.* Earth Charter International Secretariat 2000, p. 10

The art and science of teaching about, from, with, and for the Earth Charter offers a promising pedagogy for exploring such shared values and global ethics. The story of the Earth Charter itself—the commitment, the emergence of a people's charter for the twenty-first century, is compelling. It is a hopeful saga of global cross-cultural collaboration. Teaching <u>about</u> this process and its successful culmination is expository and inspiring.

Individual principles can be used too as ways of exploring issues and as a guide for further discussion of actions that are ethical and sustainable. Teaching <u>from</u> the Earth Charter on the major principles of care for life, ecological integrity, social and economic justice, and creating a culture of peace opens topics of critical importance. Individual subprinciples can be used to support, justify, and clarify concrete issues as well as contextual and related ones.

The Earth Charter in its comprehensive inclusion of social, political, economic, and environmental problems and solutions can be used for teaching the interrelatedness of these issues. Teaching <u>with</u> the Earth Charter as the content of sustainability in all its pluralism of thought can give students a conspectus of the debate. It can serve as a framework for sustainability education.

In appropriate settings, one can advocate on behalf of the principles. Teaching <u>for</u> the Earth Charter can have many aims—to connect students to the vast cosmological mystery, to find a language of reverence and humility, to contribute to the discourse of how the principles might be realized. In this way, it can serve as an invitation to participate in action.

The Rationale for an Ethical Framework

> *I am concerned that globalization has been an unguided, leaderless phenomenon that has left millions of people with no immediate apparent benefits. Yes, it has increased global wealth, but is has also diminished the value of traditional cultures and ways of life, it has opened up old wounds, and it has created a new set of injustices that breed violence as well as political and religious extremism. I am an economist, but I am convinced that we cannot go on with the pure economization of life, where everything is measured in terms of money and the capacity to generate wealth. I am convinced that humanity needs a common agreed ethical framework.* Lubbers 2001, p. 1

Increasingly, we see the global movement of money, of ideas, of people. Increasingly, we see the need for shared commitments to equity, justice, environmental integrity, and peace. Globalization, with its rapacious appetite for natural and human resources, and with its lack of democratic governing forces, must be turned to the good. If it can be, I believe it will be through finding common ground among all peoples on ways to manage global economic forces, and by creating cultural forces to insure the fundamental principles of a global community that is sustainable.

The Earth Charter is an inspiring declaration of such values. It has been influenced by philosophical traditions of secular and religious belief, the global ethics movement, international law, peoples, treaties, contemporary science, and the wisdom of diverse groups of indigenous peoples.

Surely it is not the last word on a global ethical framework, but it is an invitation to reflect on the significance of globalization for life on earth. It is also a call to consider the responsibility of the academy to raise issues related to the direction in which globalization is going. If our way of life is to be a sustainable one, if globalization is to be humane, we in higher education need to engage deeply in such challenges.

The core values of the Earth Charter, as Brendan Mackey, Director of Education for the Earth Charter has written, "are life affirming, promote human dignity, advance environmental protection and social and economic justice, and respect cultural and ecological diversity and integrity." They are an excellent place to begin. They represent serious intellectual and cultural efforts to chart a course toward global responsibility and global sustainability. How we manage globalization will determine the quality of life on Earth. Institutions of higher education, in particular, have a moral obligation to examine critically globalization and seek to move it in a direction that is humane, just, and sustainable – in the direction of good. The Earth Charter provides an ethical framework for this urgent task.

References

Earth Charter Commission (2000): The Earth Charter. Available: http://www.earthcharter.org.

Earth Charter International Secretariat (2000). Earth Charter Briefing Book. San Jose, Costa Rica.

Earth Charter International Secretariat (2001): The Earth Charter Initiative Handbook. San Jose, Costa Rica. Available: http://www.earthcharter.org/resources/publications/handbook.pdf.

Lubbers, R. (2001): Untitled address to the Nobel Peace Prize Centennial Symposium. December 6, 2001, Oslo, Norway.

Mackey, B. (2001): Update on the Earth Charter Education Programme. Earth Charter Bulletin.

Rockefeller, S.C. (2001): The Earth Charter: Building a Global Culture of Peace. Speech at the Earth Charter Community Summits, September 29, 2001, Tampa, Florida.

Hans-Peter Winkelmann

COPERNICUS-CAMPUS – The University Network for Sustainability in Europe

The COPERNICUS-Programme of the European University Association EUA (the successor of CRE), was launched by European rectors already in 1988. The acronym COPERNICUS stands for **CO**operation Programme in Europe for Research on Nature and Industry through Coordinated University Studies". The COPERNICUS programme represents an effort to mobilise the resources of universities and academia around the theme of sustainability and to support higher education institutions in the implementation of issues on sustainable development. The role of COPERNICUS has always been about what universities can do to help society meet the challenge of sustainable development. The focus of COPERNICUS has been within the university: on teachers, students and administrators, through activities centred on interdisciplinary teaching and action at institutional level. COPERNICUS is firstly a programme for higher education institutions; the members of COPERNICUS are the universities themselves.

The main instrument of COPERNICUS for furthering this commitment on part of universities is the *University Charter for Sustainable Development,* which marked a breakthrough in raising consciousness within the European universities about the necessity to work together to preserve the future. The main lines of action derived from the COPERNICUS Charter could tentatively be targeted on the learning process of individuals and at influencing the behaviour of organisations and individuals within those organisations. The aims of the COPERNICUS Charter reflect both the desire to promote a know-how transfer among higher education institutions and to identify, promote and disseminate exemplary practices and, strategies for making sustainability more central to university life in order to contribute to the European integration. This process should respect diverse approaches to sustainability in higher education. By following this mission, COPERNICUS can contribute to promoting cohesion among universities in all parts of Europe.

Today, COPERNICUS constitutes a unique network consisting of more than 300 universities in 37 European countries representing the European universities on issues of environment and sustainable development. COPERNICUS is an independent non-profit NGO under German law. The COPERNICUS secretariat stimulates universities to exchange their views and to disseminate the results achieved in higher education for sustainability.

The member universities of this network are ready to share experiences and develop together innovative approaches to sustainability in university education. The idea is for them to cooperate on the best ways to promote sustainable development and the environment as issues both within their institutions and in their relations with outside partners like business, governments and international organizations. Since the programme's inception, two areas of university life have emerged as particularly fertile for the COPERNICUS approach: (1) the area of lifelong learning, in which the productive sector often draws closer to the university and (2) the management of the university, where the capacity to foster change in attitudes and procedures is highest. These two areas are also central to the future development of most higher education institutions in Europe.

The type of activities that have been launched by COPERNICUS until now indicate that there is a market for inter-university cooperation for sustainable development. These visible products such as the 'European Virtual Seminar' or the 'European Solar Campus' are also useful 'visiting cards' to enable COPERNICUS to move ahead in the area of influencing policy.

COPERNICUS-CAMPUS as a Tool for Networking, Partnership and Community Building of Universities in Europe to Promote Sustainable Development

As described above, COPERNICUS was able to enhance very well contact between universities and institutions of higher education in Europe by establishing a flourishing network in the past. In view of the Bologna Process and the objectives to make Europe more competitive, to boost mobility and ensure quality and the promotion of excellence in science and research, it is now moving into a new phase, in which it must think of setting up an establishment for building community among universities in Europe. In order to meet the increasing demand for a more intensive and efficient level of inter-university cooperation that enables universities to collaborate in the best possible ways to promote sustainable development as a key issue within their education activities, the newly developed COPERNICUS-CAMPUS is a critical tool provided by universities for universities for networking, partnership and community building.

COPERNICUS-CAMPUS offers an inter-disciplinary trans-European community-building mechanism for a coordinated resource and information sharing among individuals, institutions and resources within the European Higher Education Area, that allows universities to learn from each other how to implement the principles of sustainable development within all relevant areas of university education. Furthermore, it strengthens the loose structure of the COPERNICUS network through the establishment of a virtual organizational structure that brings together needs-driven information matching demand with supply, thus created for the mutual benefit of all universities supporting sound decision-making. The approaches identified could be used as the basis for a more systematic look at concrete institutional integration of sustainability into higher education like the implementation of the COPERNICUS Charter principles.

The above-mentioned aims of COPERNICUS-CAMPUS reflect both the need to foster a more integrated and multidisciplinary approach to the development of a more sustainable society. This task is much broader than the traditional tasks of universities and therefore universities will have to cooperate more intensively. It becomes more and more apparent that universities must share their knowledge and expertise and to transform from "knowledge islands" into nodes in a "knowledge network". Of course each node in the network has it's own identity and its own characteristics, but draws knowledge and expertise from a much larger reservoir. The new opportunities created in the rapidly developing field of information and communication technology are highly promising in this respect. For the different client groups of modern universities this means that their learning and working environment can be much more trans-European.

In order to meet the future challenges, also universities have to share their knowledge through the development of internationally oriented networks which allow the building of new partnerships in virtual networks. COPERNICUS-CAMPUS plays the role of a "knowledge-navigator" that offers "best-practices" and expertise from universities participating in the virtual knowledge network. The target is to bring together universities within strategic partnerships on projects which are being used as virtual platforms for the solution of common problems. Such an inter-university community-building mechanism is aiming in the first place at the "empowerment" of universities.

COPERNICUS-CAMPUS focuses very much on such a sharing of knowledge through a benchmarking on this virtual platform. In general, this model should function as a networking tool for the cooperation between different European universities in order to stimulate a sharing of knowledge and expertise on higher education for sustainability.

Since sustainable development with its environmental, social and economic dimensions is a vast area, COPERNICUS-CAMPUS must focus in order to break with new ideas. In the light of the creation of an European Research Area and an European Higher Education Space, COPERNICUS-CAMPUS will therefore emphasize the following key elements of higher education for sustainability in the future:

- How can higher education contribute to sustainable development?
  - Through the generation of new knowledge (multidisciplinary research on sustainability issues)
  - By spreading of knowledge through education (integration of sustainability issues into curricula)
  - By disseminating of knowledge to society (partnerships with other stakeholders)
  - Through the sustainable management of universities ("Practice what you preach")

- What are the challenges of higher education to promote sustainable development?
  - The following themes should be considered as key dimensions for promoting sustainability through higher education:
  - Latest scientific understanding of sustainability
  - Sustainable consumption and production patterns
  - Reorientation of teacher education towards sustainable development
  - Continuing education
  - Awareness raising on sustainability issues
  - Inter-cultural exchange in the learning environment;
  - Networking among institutions of education
  - Interaction with stakeholders in the development process
  - ...

The principal activity for COPERNICUS-CAMPUS is to organize specialized projects on these core themes and to sustain university cooperation on these topics.

According to the attached model (see scheme), the COPERNICUS-CAMPUS initiative leads to a couple of action-related outputs that will support the community-building of universities in Europe by creating a collaborative learning and working environment for a better contribution of higher education for sustainable development. The envisaged outputs can boost trans-European inter-university knowledge exchange and close cooperation on sustainable development issues. They will also facilitate the creation of a new level of cooperation between the more than 300 universities as they will raise the quality and effectiveness of current approaches. It provides the universities with a comprehensive set of "university to university services" so that it becomes the key for the promotion of sustainability through higher education.

The activities and outputs of COPERNICUS-CAMPUS can be centred around the two following key areas:
1. Creation of a common knowledge base for universities on sustainability issues
2. Creation of a collaborative working environment for universities on sustainability issues

All envisaged activities are closely interrelated and are briefly described as follows:

- **COPERNICUS-CAMPUS clearinghouse mechanism**
In order to reinforce the network development COPERNICUS-CAMPUS is establishing a "clearinghouse-mechanism" that should bring together European universities in close partnerships to carry out joint activities for a sustainable development. The COPERNICUS-CAMPUS clearinghouse-mechanism will bring together information and resources on sustainability from universities all over Europe that are required for a more intensive and close networking. New information and resources are being added to the clearinghouse on a continual basis. The clearinghouse-mechanism of the COPERNICUS-CAMPUS will be based on the philosophy that broad participation and easy access must be a top priority. A channel of communication should therefore be build on modern internet-based ICT tools, such as virtual work-

ing spaces and interactive databases. This internet platform should be designed to last in a long-term view. It shall ensure a widespread dissemination within the entire higher education community inside and outside Europe and within education institutions of other levels. Furthermore it will offer a meeting place for universities and other important actors in the society such as business and industry to promote discussions and common activities of academics and professionals in economy and production. An electronic newsletter that will frequently address the universities will be of crucial importance for the network cohesion and the information transfer within the network. The clearinghouse-mechanism of the COPERNICUS-CAMPUS will be critical as information service for news, events and project proposals referring to sustainable development and will be an integral part of the community-building process.

- **Good practice-inventory on sustainability issues**

A major tool for the creation of a common knowledge base will be a comprehensive internet-based inventory of good practices on the promotion of sustainability through higher education. The COPERNICUS-CAMPUS will invite proposals in an "Open Call for Good Practices" and will identify and collect case studies on approaches for the promotion of sustainability through higher education Such a call for good practices will also include an enquiry designed to find out more about the individual background of an activity. In an additional need-analysis section, the demand for further going information and action will be identified. The good practices provide a model for action and a target oriented roadmap for others to use.

- **Dissemination of information on sustainability issues**

All submitted good practices will be grouped according the core themes of sustainability in higher education and disseminated through the comprehensive COPERNICUS-CAMPUS internet-based directory. It shall offer the European universities a comprehensive knowledge base on how to integrate sustainable development issues into courses and curricula. The collection of teaching materials and teaching methodologies shall address both disciplinary-related education and multi-/ cross-disciplinary approaches. Application of modern information and communication technology for the dissemination of knowledge will result in a more efficient European wide sharing of knowledge and expertise. Collaborative learning and knowledge-sharing using ICT-tools could reinforce the necessary international dimension in teaching European students. Such approach will enable more students and staff members to become involved in COPERNICUS-CAMPUS initiatives in a time- and cost-effective way.

- **Knowledge-sharing (Benchmarking)**

After compiling the good practice inventory, an assessment of existing approaches in higher education for sustainable development will constitute the next step. For the implementation of sustainable practices by the universities themselves, a methodology for the assessment of universities' performances both at the managerial and educational levels should be developed within the framework of the COPERNICUS-CAMPUS in order to promote the most efficient functioning in terms of awareness-raising and impacts. Comparison of methodologies practiced at European universities will result in the co-operative development of a system for good practices of integrating sustainability into higher education. Benchmarking could provide the appropriate tool for such an approach. If the outcomes of this initiative are positive, the results could subsequently be extended to other European universities. Benchmarking is more than simply comparing oneself to a statistical standard. Working and learning systematically, firstly requires to understand internal work procedures, then to search externally for "best practices" in other institutions. The type of benchmarking - or knowledge-sharing - that should be applied in higher education is different from the process in corporations. In higher education comparisons should be made among "peer institutions" more in a style of friendly rivalry. The appropriate benchmarking procedure for universities of the COPERNICUS-CAMPUS can be described therefore as learning by comparing, looking at what universities need and how others are doing it.

- **Interdisciplinary working groups on sustainability issues**

The central scheme for the creation of a collaborative working environment and for the active involvement of as many universities as possible in COPERNICUS-CAMPUS will be the establishment of interdisciplinary trans-European working groups for universities on the environmental, social and economic dimensions of sustainable development. The strategic aim of the working groups is to create a permanent and sustainable structure that will enable universities to work together in specialized projects and partnerships related to their area of expertise. To achieve a close and effective collaboration, staff and students from the COPERNICUS universities will be invited to group and form the working groups around the collected good practices within the COPERNICUS-CAMPUS framework. Further topics could be focussed according to the demand of the participating university members. Suitable ICT tools like virtual meeting places and databases of resources and contact persons linked to each topic will offer the opportunity for geographically spread collaborative work. The cohesion of the working groups will be reinforced within working group meetings that will be part of the COPERNICUS-CAMPUS conferences. Based on the good practice inventory, coherent recommendations should be cooperatively developed and added to the process of a European wide sharing of knowledge and expertise. The working groups will be coordinated within the COPERNICUS-CAMPUS similar to a "project-center" approach that should allow in the long-run also a better participation of universities in the programmes carried out on the European Union level (e.g. 6th Framework Programme, Socrates, Tempus etc.). The combined knowledge on funding programmes and suitable applicable resources channelled into the working groups will create a unique opportunity for universities in Europe to react to calls and tenders in a very efficient way, bringing together strong partners for project proposals on university levels. Examples for such collaborative project-oriented approach and a sound springboard for the future are the working groups on issues already addressed by COPERNICUS, such as on open distance learning (ODL), lifelong learning, the reorientation of teacher education or on the promotion of sustainable consumption and production patterns. The working groups will also provide an opportunity for "university to university" (U2U) consultancy. If one university has a specific problem, the working groups can explain how others have solved it. The universities will not advise each other, but they can use the COPERNICUS-CAMPUS to exchange solutions and experiences. Such consultancy by universities for universities can be accomplished also by so-called inhouse-seminars to be organized by the working groups on demand of individual universities.

- **Conferences**

To bring together all relevant groups like teachers, researchers, students and administrators for a face-to-face dialogue for a presentation and exchange of projects and experiences in the field of sustainable development, COPERNICUS-CAMPUS will organize annual conferences. The annual conferences will provide a forum for universities in Europe to discuss the progress of the project and to promote further development. The events will also give the opportunity to disseminate tentative results, both inside and outside the working groups. The working group meetings will represent an integral part of the conferences. The next COPERNICUS Conferences will be held 2003 in Pecs (Hungary).

Conclusions

COPERNICUS-CAMPUS aims at continuously extending the involvement of European higher education institutions into the creation of a common knowledge base and a collaborative working environment for the promotion of sustainable development in Europe. The steadily growing COPERNICUS network (1997: 217 members; 1999: 279; today 306 members) will play the central role for the dissemination and offers the strongest advantage of this academic network. The potential impact of the COPERNICUS-CAMPUS on the European Higher Education Area appears reasonably high in this regard.

COPERNICUS, via the institutional cooperation with the European University Association EUA and of its own initiative, is networked well throughout the continent to carry out its activities in a coherent and effective manner. As already mentioned, more than 300 higher education institutions in 37 European countries are members of the continuously growing COPERNICUS network. The EUA represents more than 620 individual, collective and affiliate members, located in 45 countries: higher education institutions, national rector's conference and national associations of other higher education institutions, finally regional and international associations and networks, as well as interuniversity institutions.

The most important means to create a "European Area of Knowledge for Sustainability" is to involve EUA members and other higher education institutions into the annual COPERNICUS-CAMPUS conference and invite them to participate actively in a structured, continuous and lasting cooperation within projects launched in the framework of the COPERNICUS-CAMPUS.

Ways to Institutionalize the Concepts 231

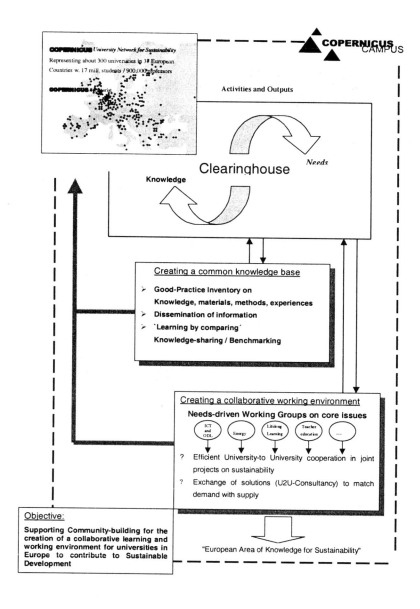

**Programmes,
Priority Areas,
Projects...**

...aiming at the incorporation of sustainability
into the European Higher Education Area

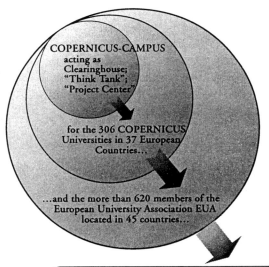

COPERNICUS-CAMPUS
acting as
Clearinghouse;
"Think Tank";
"Project Center"

for the 306 COPERNICUS
Universities in 37 European
Countries...

...and the more than 620 members of the
European University Association EUA
located in 45 countries...

...supporting community-building for the creation
of a collaborative learning and working environment for
universities in Europe and contributes to the

"European Higher Education Area for Sustainability"
with impact on...
...more than 17 Mio students,
...more than 900,000 professors,
university administrators, researchers

European
University
Association
EUA

COPERNICUS
– List of Members –
(as of 31st August 2002)

Albania:
University of Tirana, Tirana

Austria:
Karl-Franzens-Universität Graz, Graz
Leopold-Franzens-Universität, Innsbruck
Universität Klagenfurt, Klagenfurt
Johannes Kepler Universität Linz, Linz
Universität Wien, Wien
Universität für Bodenkultur Wien, Wien
Universität für Musik und Darstellende Kunst, Wien
Veterinärmedizinische Universität Wien, Wien

Belgium:
Universitaire Centrum Antwerpen, Antwerpen
Universitaire Faculteiten Sint-Ignatius, Antwerpen
Universitaire Instelling Antwerpen, Antwerpen
University of Antwerpen, Antwerpen
Vrije Universiteit Brussel, Brussel
Université Libre de Bruxelles, Bruxelles
Universiteit Gent, Gent
Katholieke Universiteit Leuven, Leuven
Université de Liège, Liège
Université Catholique de Louvain, Louvain-la-Neuve
Faculté Polytechnique de Mons, Mons
Université de Mons-Hainaut, Mons
Facultés Universitaires Notre Dame de la Paix, Namur

Bosnia and Herzegovina:
University of Sarajevo, Sarajevo
The University of Tuzla, Tuzla

Bulgaria:
Academy of Medicine, Sofia
University of Architecture Civil Engineering & Geodesy, Sofia
Technical University of Sofia, Sofia
University of National and World Economy, Sofia
Université Saint Kliment Ohridski, Sofia

Croatia:
Josip Juraj Strossmayer University, Osijek
University of Zagreb, Zagreb

Czech Republic:
University of Veterinary and Pharmaceutical Sciences, Brno
The University of Technology, Brno
Czech Technical University, Praha
Université Charles, Praha

Denmark:
Aalborg Universitetscenter, Aalborg
Technical University of Denmark, Lyngby
Roskilde Universitetscenter, Roskilde

Estonia:
University of Tartu, Tartu

Finland:
Åbo Akademi University, Åbo
College of Veterinary Medicine, Helsinki
Helsinki School of Economics and Business Administration, Helsinki
University of Helsinki, Helsinki
University of Industrial Arts, Helsinki
Swedish School of Economics and Business Administration, Helsinki
University of Joensuu, Joensuu
University of Jyväskylä, Jyväskylä
Kymenlaasko Polytechnic, Kotka

University of Kuopio, Kuopio
University of Oulu, Oulu
University of Lapland, Rovaniemi
University of Tampere, Tampere
Turku School of Economics and Business Administration, Turku
University of Vaasa, Vaasa

France:
Université d'Angers, Angers
Université Bordeaux 1, Talence
Université de Savoie, Chambéry
Université de Technologie de Compiègne, Compiègne
Université Catholique de Lille, Lille
Université Claude Bernard – Lyon 1, Lyon/Villeurbanne
Université de Metz, Metz
Université Paris VII, Paris
Université de Vincennes à St-Denis – Paris 8, Paris
Université de Paris IV – Sorbonne, Paris
Université de Paris XII - Val de Marne, Paris
Université de Perpignan, Perpignan
Université de Rennes 2 – Haute Bretagne, Rennes
Université Robert Schuman de Strasbourg, Strasbourg
Université Paul Sabatier – Toulouse III, Toulouse

Germany:
Universität Augsburg, Augsburg
Otto-Friedrich-Universität, Bamberg
Freie Universität Berlin, Berlin
Humboldt-Universität, Berlin
Technische Universität Berlin, Berlin
Universität Bielefeld, Bielefeld
Universität Bremen, Bremen
Brandenburgische Technische Universität Cottbus, Cottbus
Technische Universität Darmstadt, Darmstadt
Universität Dortmund, Dortmund
Universität-Gesamthochschule-Duisburg, Duisburg
Katholische Universität Eichstätt, Eichstätt
Universität Essen, Essen
Justus-Liebig-Universität, Giessen
Technische Universität Hamburg-Harburg, Hamburg
Universität Hamburg, Hamburg
Universität Hannover, Hannover
Universität Hildesheim, Hildesheim
Universität Hohenheim, Stuttgart
Technische Universität Ilmenau, Ilmenau
Universität Kaiserslautern, Kaiserslautern
Universität Karlsruhe, Karlsruhe
Universität-Gesamthochschule Kassel, Kassel
Christian-Albrechts-Universität zu Kiel, Kiel
Deutsche Sporthochschule Köln, Köln
Universität Leipzig, Leipzig
Universität Lüneburg, Lüneburg
Carl V. Ossietzky Universität Oldenburg, Oldenburg
Universität Osnabrück, Osnabrück
Universität Regensburg, Regensburg
Universität Rostock, Rostock
Fachhochschule Rottenburg, Rottenburg
Universität des Saarlandes, Saarbrücken
Universität-Gesamthochschule, Siegen
Fachhochschule Trier
Universität Trier, Trier
University of Ulm, Ulm/Donau
Bergische Universität-Gesamthochschule Wuppertal, Wuppertal
Bayerische Julius-Maximilians-Universität, Würzburg
Hochschule Zittau/Görlitz, Zittau
Internationales Hochschulinstitut IHI Zittau

Greece:
National Technical University of Athens, Athinai
Athens University of Economics and Business, Athinai

University of Ioannina, Ioannina
Democritus University of Thrace, Komotini
University of Patras, Patras
University of Macedonia Economic and Social Sciences, Thessaloniki
Aristotle University of Thessaloniki, Thessaloniki

Hungary:
Budapest University of Economic Sciences, Budapest
Central European University, Budapest
Technical University of Budapest, Budapest
University of Veterinary Science, Budapest
Agricultural University of Debrecen, Debrecen
Kossuth Lajos University, Debrecen
Gödöllö University of Agriculture, Gödöllö
Janus Pannonius University, Pécs
Jozsef Atilla University, Szeged
University of Veszprém, Veszprém

Ireland:
Dublin City University, Dublin
Trinity College, Dublin
University College Galway, Galway
University of Limerick, Limerick

Island:
University of Iceland, Reykjavik

Italy:
Università degli Studi di Ancona, Ancona
Università degli Studi di Bologna, Bologna
University of Catania, Catania
Università degli Studi "G. d'Annunzio", Chieti
Università degli Studi di Firenze, Firenze
Istituto Universitario Europeo, S. Domenico di Fiesole
Politecnico di Milano, Milano
Università degli Studi di Modena, Modena
Università degli Studi di Padova, Padova
Università degli Studi di Siena, Siena
Politecnico di Torino, Torino
Università degli Studi di Trieste
Universita degli Studi di Udine, Udine
Università degli Studi di Venezia, Venezia

Latvia:
University of Latvia, Riga

Lithuania:
Kaunas University of Technology, Kaunas

Former Yougoslav Republic of Macedonia/F.Y.R.O.M:
"St.Kiril and Metodij" University, Skopje

Malta:
University of Malta, Msida

Moldova:
State Agrarian University of Moldova, Chisinau

The Netherlands:
Universiteit van Amsterdam, Amsterdam
Vrije Universiteit, Amsterdam
Delft University of Technology, Delft
Eindhoven University of Technology, Eindhoven
Universiteit Twente, Enschede
Rijksuniversiteit Groningen, Groningen
Open Universiteit, Heerlen
Rijksuniversiteit te Leiden, Leiden
Universiteit Maastricht, Maastricht
Katholieke Universiteit Nijmegen, Nijmegen
Erasmus Universiteit Rotterdam, Rotterdam
Katholieke Universiteit Brabant, Tilburg
Rijksuniversiteit te Utrecht, Utrecht

Wageningen Agricultural University, Wageningen

Norway:
University of Bergen, Bergen
University of Oslo, Oslo
Norwegian University of Science and Technology (NTNU)

Poland:
University of Gdansk, Gdansk
Technical University of Gdansk, Gdansk
Technical University of Silesia, Gliwice
Karkonoshe College, Jelenia Gora
University of Silesia, Katowice
Stanislav Staszic University of Mining & Metallurgy, Kraków
The Jagiellonian University, Kraków
Technical University of Lódz, Lódz
University of Lódz, Lódz
Marie Curie-Sklodowska University, Lublin
Olsztyn University of Agriculture and Technology, Olsztyn
Adam Mickiewicz University, Poznan
Uniwersytet Mikolaja Kopernika, Torun
Warsaw University of Technology, Warszawa
University of Warsaw, Warszawa
Warsaw School of Economics, Warszawa
University of Wroclaw, Wroclaw
Technical University of Wroclaw, Wroclaw

Portugal:
Universidade do Minho, Braga
Universidade Catolica Portuguesa, Lisboa
Universidade Nova de Lisboa, Lisboa
Universidade Técnica de Lisboa, Lisboa
Universidade de Lisboa, Lisboa
Universidade do Porto, Porto

Romania:
Université "Trasilvania" Brasov, Brasov
Polytechnic Institute of Bucharest, Bucuresti
University of Bucharest, Bucuresti
Babes-Bolyai University, Cluj-Napoca
University of Medicine and Pharmacy, Cluj-Napoca
University of Craiova, Craiova
"Politehnica" University of Timisoara, Timisoare

Russia:
Kaliningrad State University, Kaliningrad
Novosibirsk State Technical University, Novosibirsk
St. Petersburg University, St. Petersburg

Slovak Republic:
Comenius University, Bratislava
Slovak University of Technology, Bratislava

Slovenia:
University of Ljubljana, Ljubljana
University of Maribor, Maribor

Spain:
University of Alicante, Alicante
Universidad de Extramadura, Badajoz
Universitat Autónoma de Barcelona, Barcelona
Universitat de Barcelona, Barcelona
Universitat Politècnica de Catalunya, Barcelona
Universidad de Cádiz, Cádiz
Universidad de Castilla-La Mancha, Ciudad Real
University of Girona, Girona
Universidad de Granada, Granada
Universidad Autonoma de Madrid, Madrid
Universidad Complutense de Madrid, Madrid
Universidad Politécnica de Madrid, Madrid
Universidad Pontificia Comillas de Madrid, Madrid

Ways to Institutionalize the Concepts — 237

Universidad Nacional de Educación a Distanzia (UNED), Madrid
Universidad de Málaga, Málaga
Universidad de Murcia, Murcia
Universidad de Las Palmas de Gran Canaria, Las Palmas/Gran Canaria
Universidad de Navarra, Pamplona
Universidad Pontificia de Salamanca, Salamanca
Universidad de Salamanca, Salamanca
Universidad de Cantabria, Santander
Universidad de Santiago de Compostela, Santiago de Compostela
Universitat Rovira i Vergili, Tarragona
Universitat de Valencia, Valencia
Universidad de Valladolid, Valladolid
Universidad de Zaragoza, Zaragoza

Sweden:
University College of Borås, Borås
University of Gävle, Gävle
Chalmers University of Technology, Göteborg
University of Göteborg, Göteborg
Karlstad University, Karlstad
Linköping University & Institute of Technology, Linköping
Lunds University, Lund
Malmö University, Malmö
Stockholm School of Economics, Stockholm
The Royal Institute of Technology, Stockholm
University of Stockholm, Stockholm
Umea University, Umea
Swedish University of Agricultural Sciences, Uppsala
University of Uppsala, Uppsala
Mälardalen University, Västeras

Switzerland:
Université de Fribourg, Fribourg
University of Geneva, Geneva
Ecole Polytechnique Fédérale de Lausanne, Lausanne
Université de Lausanne, Lausanne
ETH Zürich (Hochschule), Zürich
Universität Zürich, Zürich

Turkey:
Ankara Üniversitesi, Ankara
Hacettepe University, Ankara
Middle East Technical University, Ankara
Uludag Üniversitesi, Bursa
Trakya Üniversitesi, Edirne
T.C. Anadolu Üniversitesi, Eskisehir
Bogaziçi Üniversitesi, Istanbul
Marmara Üniversitesi, Istanbul
Yildiz Technical University, Istanbul
Ege Üniversitesi, Izmir
Ondokuz Mayis Üniversitesi, Samsun

Ukraine:
Kiev T.G. Shevchenko State University, Kiev
Odessa State Academy of Refrigeration, Odessa
Odessa State Polytechnic University, Odessa
Odessa State University, Odessa
Odessa State Maritime University

United Kingdom:
The Queen's University of Belfast, Belfast
University of Sussex, Brighton
University of Bristol, Bristol
University of Cambridge, Cambridge
University of Kent at Canterbury, Canterbury
University of Ulster, Coleraine
University of Abertay Dundee, Dundee
University of Durham, Durham
Heriot-Watt University, Edinburgh
University of Strathclyde, Glasgow
University of Glasgow, Glasgow
University of Surrey, Guildford
University of Hertfordshire, Hatfield
University of Huddersfield, Huddersfield

Kingston University, Kingston upon Thames
University of Wales, Lampeter
University of Leeds, Leeds
De Montfort University, Leicester
Liverpool John Moores University, Liverpool
University of East London, London
Middlesex University, London
University of Westminster, London
University of Northumbria at Newcastle, Newcastle upon Tyne
The Nottingham Trent University, Nottingham
University of Portsmouth, Portsmouth
University of Central Lancashire, Preston
Staffordshire University, Stafford
University of Stirling, Stirling
University of Sunderland, Sunderland
University of Wolverhampton, Wolverhampton

Vatican:
Università Pontificia Salesiana, Roma

Yugoslavia:
Univerzitet "Svetozar Markovíc", Kragujevac
Univerzitet u Nisu, Nis

Others:
Conselho de Reitores das Universidades Portuguesas, Lisbon
DAAD, Bonn
Department of Linguistics applied to Science & Technology
Stuurgroep Handvest Duurzaamheid HBO, Utrecht

TOTAL   306

Appendix

The role of universities in agenda 21

In the following chapters of Agenda 21 universities and other higher education institutions are urged to contribute to sustainable development in a concrete way:

SECTION I. SOCIAL AND ECONOMIC DIMENSIONS

Chapter 6:
"Protecting and promoting human health"

SECTION II. CONSERVATION AND MANAGEMENT OF
RESOURCES FOR DEVELOPMENT

Chapter 8:
"Integrating environment and development in decision-making"

Chapter 10:
"Integrated approach to the planning and management of land resources"

Chapter 11:
"Combating desertification"

Chapter 16:
"Environmentally sound management of biotechnology"

SECTION III. STRENGTHENING THE ROLE OF MAJOR GROUPS

Chapter 31:
"Scientific and technological community"

SECTION IV. MEANS OF IMPLEMENTATION

Chapter 35:
"Science for sustainable development"

Chapter 36:
"Promoting education, public awareness and training"

Chapter 37:
"National mechanisms and international cooperation for capacity-building in developing countries"

Declarations on Sustainability in Universities

A. COPERNICUS UNIVERSITY CHARTER FOR SUSTAINABLE DEVELOPMENT
(European University Association EUA)

Preamble

Man's exploitation of the biosphere is now threatening its very existence and delicate balance. Over the last few decades, the pressures on the global environment have become self-evident, leading to a common outcry for sustainable development. In the words of the Brundtland report, we must learn to care for the needs of the present without compromising the ability of future generations everywhere to meet their own needs.

The awareness is there. What is required is a comprehensive strategy for building a sustainable future which is equitable for all human beings, as highlighted by the Rio Conference (UNCED) in 1992. This requires a new frame of mind and new sets of values.

Education is critical for promoting such values and improving people's capacity to address environment and development issues. Education at all levels, especially university education for the training of decision-makers and teachers, should be oriented towards sustainable development and foster environmentally aware attitudes, skills and behavior patterns, as well as a sense of ethical responsibility. Education must become environmental education in the fullest sense of the term.

The role of universities

Universities and equivalent institutions of higher education train the coming generations of citizens and have expertise in all fields of research, both in technology as well as in the natural, human and social sciences. It is consequently their duty to propagate environmental literacy and to promote the practice of environmental ethics in society, in accordance with the principles set out in the Magna Chart of European Universities and subsequent university declarations, and along the lines of the UNCED recommendations for environment and development education.

Indeed, universities are increasingly called upon to play a leading role in developing a multidisciplinary and ethically-oriented form of education in order to devise solutions for the problems linked to sustainable development. They must therefore commit themselves to an on-going process of informing, educating and mobilizing all the relevant parts of society concerning the consequences of ecological degradation, including its impact on global development and the conditions needed to ensure a sustainable and just world.

To achieve these aims and fulfill their basic mission, universities are urged to make every effort to subscribe to and implement the ten principles of actions set out below.

Principles of action

1. Institutional commitment
Universities shall demonstrate real commitment to the principle and practice of environmental protection and sustainable development within the academic milieu.

2. Environmental ethics
Universities shall promote among teaching staff, students and the public at large sustainable consumption patterns and an ecological lifestyle, while fostering programmes to develop the capacities of the academic staff to teach environmental literacy.

3. Education of university employees
Universities shall provide education, training and encouragement to their employees on environmental issues, so that they can pursue their work in an environmentally responsible manner.

4. Programmes in environmental education
Universities shall incorporate an environmental perspective in all their work and set up environmental education programmes involving both teachers and researchers as well as students - all of whom should be exposed to the global challenges of environment and development, irrespective of their field of study.

5. Interdisciplinarity
Universities shall encourage interdisciplinary and collaborative education and research programmes related to sustainable development as part of the institution's central mission. Universities shall also seek to overcome competitive instincts between disciplines and departments.

6. Dissemination of knowledge
Universities shall support efforts to fill in the gaps in the present literature available for students, professionals, decision-makers and the general public by preparing information didactic material, organizing public lectures, and establishing training programmes. They should also be prepared to participate in environmental audits.

7. Networking
Universities shall promote interdisciplinary networks of environmental experts at the local, national, regional and international levels, with the aim of collaborating on common environmental projects in both research and education. For this, the mobility of students and scholars should be encouraged.

8. Partnerships
Universities shall take the initiative in forging partnerships with other concerned sectors of society, in order to design and implement coordinated approaches, strategies and action plans.

9. Continuing education programmes
Universities shall devise environmental educational programmes on these issues for different target groups: e.g. business, governmental agencies, non-governmental organizations, the media.

10. Technology transfer
Universities shall contribute to educational programmes designed to transfer educationally sound and innovative technologies and advanced management methods.

This document is a follow-up to a number of university initiatives concerned with environmental awareness and responsibility, recent examples of which include:
- the Magna Charta of European Universities, Bologna, September 1988
- University Presidents for a Sustainable Future, the Talloires Declaration, October 1990
- Urgent Appeal from the CRE, the association of European universities, presented to the Preparatory Committee for the United Nations Conference on Environment and Development (UNCED), Geneva, August 1991
- Creating a Common Future: An Action Plan for Universities, Halifax, December 1991

B. THE KYOTO DECLARATION
(International Association of Universities IAU)

1. To urge universities world-wide to seek, establish and disseminate a clearer understanding of Sustainable Development – "development which meets the needs of the present without compromising the needs of future generations" – and encourage more appropriate sustainable development principles and practices at the local, national and global levels, in ways consistent with their missions.
2. To utilize resources of the university to encourage a better understanding on the part of Governments and the public at large of the inter-related physical, biological and social dangers facing the planet Earth, and to recognise the significant interdependence and international dimensions of sustainable development.

3. To emphasize the ethical obligation of the present generation to overcome those practices of resource utilisation and those widespread disparities which lie at the root of environmental unsustainability.
4. To enhance the capacity of the university to teach and undertake research and action in society in sustainable development principles, to increase environmental literacy, and to enhance the understanding of environmental ethics within the university and with the public at large.
5. To cooperate with one another and with all segments of society in the pursuit of practical and policy measures to achieve sustainable development and thereby safeguard the interests of future generations.
6. To encourage universities to review their own operations to reflect best sustainable development practices.
7. To request the IAU Administrative Board to consider and implement the ways and means to give life to this Declaration in the mission of each of its members and through the common enterprise of the IAU.

In adopting this Declaration, delegates underlined specifically the following points:
1. That sustainable development must not be interpreted in a manner that would lead to "sustained undevelopment" for certain systems, thus blocking their legitimate aspiration to raise their standard of living.
2. That sustainable development must take into consideration existing disparities in consumption and distribution patterns, with unsustainable over-consumption in some parts of the world contrasting with dramatic states of depravation in others.
3. That global sustainable development implies changes of existing value systems, a task UN which universities have an essential mission, in order to create the necessary international consciousness and global sense of responsibility and solidarity.
4. That university cooperation for sustainable development must also assure that universities from countries with insufficient proper resources may play an active role in the process.
5. That IAU, through the intellectual and organisational potential of the Association, its clearinghouse, catalyst and network function, has a major role to play in the implementation of this Declaration.

Draft Action Plan for Individual Universities

While each University can and should make its own unique contribution, an effective plan of action (IAU undertakes the initiative to "strongly encourage IAU Member Universities to adopt an institutional action plan for sustainable development) could have the following principles embodied in it. The International Association of Universities can be a clearing house and a co-ordinating expression and institutional support for its goals.

Each University, in its own action plan, will strive:
1. to make an institutional commitment to the principle and practice of sustainable development within the academic milieu and to communicate that commitment to its students, its employees and to the public at large;
2. to promote sustainable consumption practices in its own operations;
3. to develop the capacities of its academic staff to teach environmental literacy;
4. to encourage among both staff and students an environmental perspective, whatever the field of study;
5. to utilise the intellectual resources of the university to build strong environmental education programs;
6. to encourage interdisciplinary and collaborative research programs related to sustainable development as part of the institution's central mission and to overcome traditional barriers between discipline's and departments;
7. to emphasize the ethical obligations of the immediate university community - current students, faculty and staff - to understand and defeat the forces that lead to environmental degradation, North-South disparities, and the inter-generational inequities; to work at ways that will help its academic community, and the graduates, friends and governments that support it, to accept these ethical obligations;
8. to promote interdisciplinary networks of environmental experts at the local, national and international level in order to disseminate knowledge and to collaborate on common environmental projects in both research and education;
9. to promote the mobility of staff and students as essential to the free trade of knowledge;
10. to forge partnerships with other sectors of society in transferring innovative and appropriate technologies that can benefit and enhance sustainable development practices.

C. The Talloires Declaration
(University Leaders for a Sustainable Future ULSF)

We, the presidents, rectors, and Vice-Chancellors of universities from all regions of the world are deeply concerned about the unprecedented scale and speed of environmental pollution and degradation, and the depletion of natural resources.

Local, regional, and global air pollution; accumulation and distribution of toxic wastes; destruction and depletion of forests, soil, and water; depletion of the ozone layer and emission of "green house" gases threaten the survival of humans and thousands of other living species, the integrity of the earth and its biodiversity, the security of nations, and the heritage of future generations. These environmental changes are caused by inequitable and unsustainable production and consumption patterns that aggravate poverty in many regions of the world.

We believe that urgent actions are needed to address these fundamental problems and reverse the trends. Stabilization of human population, adoption of environmentally sound industrial and agricultural technologies, reforestation, and ecological restoration are crucial elements in creating an equitable and sustainable future for all humankind in harmony with nature.

Universities have a major role in the education, research, policy formation, and information exchange necessary to make these goals possible. The university heads must provide the leadership and support to mobilize internal and external resources so that their institutions respond to this urgent challenge.

We, therefore, agree to take the following actions:

1. Increase Awareness of Environmentally Sustainable Development
Use every opportunity to raise public, government, industry, foundation, and university awareness by openly addressing the urgent need to move toward an environmentally sustainable future.

2. Create an Institutional Culture of Sustainability
Encourage all universities to engage in education, research, policy formation, and information exchange on population, environment, and development to move toward global sustainability.

3. Educate for Environmentally Responsible Citizenship
Establish programs to produce expertise in environmental management, sustainable economic development, population, and related fields to ensure that all university graduates are environmentally literate and have the awareness and understanding to be ecologically responsible citizens.

4. Foster Environmental Literacy For All
Create programs to develop the capability of university faculty to teach environmental literacy to all undergraduate, graduate, and professional students.

5. Practice Institutional Ecology
Set an example of environmental responsibility by establishing institutional ecology policies and practices of resource conservation, recycling, waste reduction, and environmentally sound operations.

6. Involve All Stakeholders
Encourage involvement of government, foundations, and industry in supporting interdisciplinary research, education, policy formation, and information exchange in environmentally sustainable development. Expand work with community and nongovernmental organizations to assist in finding solutions to environmental problems.

7. Collaborate for Interdisciplinary Approaches
Convene university faculty and administrators with environmental practitioners to develop interdisciplinary approaches to curricula, research initiatives, operations, and outreach activities that support an environmentally sustainable future.

8. Enhance Capacity of Primary and Secondary Schools
Establish partnerships with primary and secondary schools to help develop the capacity for interdisciplinary teaching about population, environment, and sustainable development.

9. Broaden Service and Outreach Nationally and Internationally
Work with national and international organizations to promote a worldwide university effort toward a sustainable future.

10. Maintain the Movement
Establish a Secretariat and a steering committee to continue this momentum, and to inform and support each other's efforts in carrying out this declaration.

D. THE LÜNEBURG DECLARATION ON HIGHER EDUCATION FOR SUSTAINABLE DEVELOPMENT
of 10 October 2001

Education in all its forms plays an indispensable role in addressing the critical challenges of sustainable development. The interconnected issues of globalization, poverty alleviation, social justice, democracy, human rights, peace and environmental protection require inclusive partnerships to create a global learning environment.

Higher education has a catalyst role vis-à-vis education for sustainable development and the building of a Learning Society. It has a special responsibility to conduct the scholarship and scientific research necessary to generate the new knowledge needed and train the leaders and teachers of tomorrow, as well as communicate this knowledge to decision-makers and the public-at-large.

The ultimate goal of education for sustainable development is to impart the knowledge, values, attitudes and skills needed to empower people to bring about the changes required to achieve sustainability. Quality education for sustainable development needs to be based on state of the art knowledge and to continually review and update curricula and teaching materials accordingly. It needs to serve teachers, other professionals and all citizens as life long learners to respond to society's challenges and opportunities, so that people everywhere can live in freedom from want and fear, and to make their unique contribution to a sustainable future.

In October 2001, a conference on "Higher Education for Sustainability: Towards the World Summit on Sustainable Development 2002", was held at the University of Lüneburg, Germany. The conference was jointly organized by the University of Lüneburg and the COPERNICUS Programme of the European University Association (EUA) and was sponsored by the Global Higher Education for Sustainability Partnership (GHESP) formed by COPERNICUS, the International Association of Universities (IAU), the Association of University Leaders for a Sustainable Future (ULSF) and the United Nations Educational, Scientific and Cultural Organization (UNESCO).

GHESP partner organizations and the experts in attendance at this conference endorse the following:

1. Taking into account the recommendations and results of:
   - UNCED: Chapter 36 of Agenda 21 (1992);
   - The International Work Programme on Education, Public Awareness and Training for Sustainability adopted by the UN Commission on Sustainable Development (1996);
   - International Conference on Environment and Society (Thessaloniki, 1997);
   - World Conference on Higher Education (Paris, 1998);
   - World Conference on Science (Budapest, 1999);
   - World Education Forum (Education for All) (Dakar, 2002); and

2. Building upon the significant networks of the three academic associations which founded GHESP, beginning with over 1000 colleges and universities which pledged to implement comprehensive sustainable development action steps by signing the charters and declarations sponsored by these three organizations;

3. Calls on *higher education institutions, NGO's and other stakeholders* to:
   a. Ensure the continual review and updating of learning materials to reflect the latest scientific understanding of sustainability;
   b. Ensure that the reorientation of teacher education towards sustainable development continue to be given priority as a key component of higher education;
   c. Provide continuing education to teachers, decision makers and the public at large on sustainable development;
   d. Encourage all educational institutions to include in their activities a strong component of reflection on values and norms with respect to sustainable development;
   e. Raise awareness and increase understanding of the importance and relevance of technology assessments and risk assessment;
   f. Promote the creative development and implementation of comprehensive sustainability projects in higher education, and all other levels and forms of education;
   g. Increase attention to the international dimension and provide more opportunities for inter-cultural exchange in the learning environment;
   h. Increase a focus on capacity development and intensified networking among institutions of education; and

i. Promote stronger integration of training and research and closer interaction with stakeholders in the development process.

4. Calls on **governments** to ensure that the World Summit on Sustainable Development includes education in general, and higher education in particular, in the future international programme of work.

5. Calls upon the **United Nations** to:
   a. highlight in the Secretary-General's main policy report the indispensable role of education in general, and higher education in particular, in achieving sustainable development as stated in chapter 36 of Agenda 21.
   b. to make education a discussion topic during the multi-stakeholder dialogue sessions to be held during the preparatory committee meetings for the Johannesburg Summit and during the Summit itself.

6. Calls on **UNESCO** as task manager for chapter 36 of Agenda 21, in cooperation with UNU and other relevant parts of the United Nations system, to support these efforts concerning the Johannesburg Summit.

7. Furthermore, the EUA-COPERNICUS, the International Association of Universities (IAU), and the Association of University Leaders for a Sustainable Future (ULSF) commit to achieving the following targets within next five years:
   a. Create a global learning environment for higher education for sustainable development;
   b. Promote expanded endorsement and full implementation of the Talloires, Kyoto and Copernicus declarations;
   c. Produce an action-oriented Toolkit for universities, managers, administrators, faculty and students designed to move from commitment to concrete action. The Tool Kit would include:
      – implementation strategies for colleges and universities depending on size, type, demographic characteristics, etc.;
      – strategies for reform in particular areas of university activity, including teaching, research, operations and outreach, or for comprehensive change across all universities activities;
      – an inventory of available resources;
      – an inventory of best practices and compilation of case studies;
   d. Enhance the development of Regional Centres of excellence in both developed and developing countries, and effective networking among them.

The Lüneburg Declaration on Higher Education for Sustainable Development was adopted on 10 October 2001 in Lüneburg, Germany, on the occasion of the International COPERNICUS Conference "Higher Education for Sustainability – Towards the World Summit on Sustainable Development (Rio+10)" held at the University of Lüneburg 8–10 October 2001.

The Global Higher Education for Sustainability Partnership (GHESP)

Four international organisations with a strong commitment to making sustainability a major focus of higher education have recently formed a

> "Global Higher Education for Sustainability Partnership (GHESP)"
> Global Alliance to promote higher education for sustainable development

The four founding partners of the initiative:
- the International Association of Universities (IAU : www.unesco.org/iau),
- the University Leaders for a Sustainable Future (ULSF: www.ulsf.org/),
- COPERNICUS-CAMPUS (www.copernicus-campus.org/)
- UNESCO

combine forces in an unique effort to mobilise universities and higher education institutions to support sustainable development in response to Chapter 36 of *Agenda 21* (www.unep.org/Documents/) GHESP was formed in 2000, when the three university organisations (ULSF, IAU, COPERNICUS-CAMPUS) and UNESCO signed a first *Memorandum of Understanding* in December 2000 to collaborate and undertake joint actions in the area of higher education and sustainable development. GHESP has been formed as a result of the work program of the CSD and in anticipation of the WSSD. The partnership will be renewed for a further five year period (as of Sept 2002) in order to implement a concrete and renewed Action Plan.

The four founding partners of the initiative aim at mobilizing universities and higher education institutions around the world to support sustainable development:
- COPERNICUS-CAMPUS is responsible for the *University Charter for Sustainable Development*, signed to date by 304 university heads in 37 European countries;
- ULSF serves as the Secretariat of the 273 signatories of the *Talloires Declaration* in over 40 countries, and promotes education for sustainability based on the Earth Charter;
- IAU provides a global Forum for cooperation and a clearing house for information among more than 600 member universities and institutions of higher education which have formally adopted the *Kyoto Declaration on Sustainable Development*;
- UNESCO is the task manager for the implementation of Chapter 36 of *Agenda 21* (*Education, Public Awareness and Training*) and for the international work programme on education of the United Nations Commission on Sustainable Development, as well as the convener, in 1998, of the World Conference on Higher Education, both of which have called for the renewal of higher education to address the complex societal challenges of the 21st century.

Together, GHESP has rallied around *the Lüneburg Declaration on Higher Education for Sustainable Development* which was a milestone of the organisations' preparations for the World Summit on Sustainable Development and sets out its collective commitment to action.

The **rationale for the partnership** is the consensus that higher education must play a central role within the overall process of achieving sustainable development. The partners are convinced that if the leaders of higher education institutions and their academic colleagues in all disciplines do not make sustainability a central academic and organisational focus, it will be impossible to create a just, equitable and sustainable future. This includes the generation and dissemination of knowledge through interdisciplinary research and teaching, policy-making, capacity-building, and technology transfer. It is critical that higher education institutions understand and accept their responsibility within the broader context of social and economic development, and the building of democratic, equitable and ecologically-minded societies.

The objectives of the partnership are to:

1. Promote better understanding, and more effective implementation of strategies for the incorporation of sustainability in universities and other higher education institutions, beginning with signatories to the charters and declarations sponsored by the partner organisations; emphasis is put on the need for interdisciplinary approach in teaching and research;

2. Undertake a global review and assessment of progress in making sustainability central to curriculum, research, outreach and operations in institutions of higher education. In so doing, assist Unesco in its role within the UN system with respect to education and in line with commitments made within the follow-up of the World Conference on Higher Education;

3. Identify, share and disseminate widely, via internet, in print, through seminars and other, effective strategies, models and good practices for promoting higher education for sustainability;

4. Analyse experience thus far, with a view to making recommendations based on these studies in consultation with key stakeholders from North and South, including business, governments, other UN bodies such as the United Nations University (UNU), as well as other relevant non-governmental organisations;

5. Demonstrate that it is possible to form a partnership of non-governmental organisations working closely with the UN system to develop and implement a joint action plan addressed to achieve common goals; and analyse and evaluate this experience as an international demonstration project.

Appendix

First outcomes: Please visit the following site to access the documents online www.unesco.org/iau/ghesp/index.html :
- Memorandum of understanding
- Action Plan
- Lüneburg Declarationon on Higher Education for Sustainable Development
- Joint publication IAU/ULSF Journals, in "Higher Education Policy" (HEP 2, June 2002) on the theme *Sustainability and Higher Education : Initiatives and Agendas*
- GHESP Meeting and follow-up Conference to the WSSD to be held in Quebec City, Canada on September 21st 2002: a new *Memorandum of Understanding* will be signed and a new *Action Plan* will be defined and adopted for the next 5 years to also prepare for the *Decade of Education for Sustainable Development*.

For further information, please contact:

Eva Egron-Polak, Secretary General
International Association of Universities
Incoming GHESP Chair as of Sept. 21 2002
UNESCO House, 1, rue Miollis
75732 Paris 15, FRANCE
Tel: +33 1 45 68 45 69
Fax: +33 1 47 34 76 05
E-mail: iau@unesco.org

Richard M. Clugston,
Director University Leaders for a Sustainable Future
GHESP Chair
2100L Street, NW Washington, DC 20037 USA
Tel: 202/778 6133
Fax: 202/778 6138
E-mail: Rmclugston@aol.com

Jeanne Damlamian
Transdisciplinary Project:
Educating for a Sustainable Future
UNESCO
1, rue Miollis
75732 Paris 15, FRANCE

Tel.: +33 1 45 68 45 69
Fax: +33 1 45 68 58 30
E-mail: j.damlamian@unesco.org

Hans-Peter Winkelmann
Secretary-General,
COPERNICUS-CAMPUS Secretariat
Brandschachtstrasse 2
44149 Dortmund, GERMANY
Tel.: +49 231- 65 24 24
Fax: +49 231- 65 24 65
E-mail: hpw@copernicus-campus.org

About the Authors

Bargellini, Camilla, Milan University, Italy.

Bonnemaire, Joseph, Animal Science, ENESAD, INRA, Paris, France.

Brookes, Fiona, Higher Education Partnership for Sustainability, London, UK.

Buckland, Heloise, Higher Education Partnership for Sustainability, London, UK.

Calder, Wynn, Association of University Leaders for a Sustainable Future (ULSF) and the Center for Respect of Life and Environment (CRLE), Washington, DC, USA.

Chadœuf, Joël, Laboratory of Biometry, INRA, Paris, France.

Chevre, Anne-Marie, UMR of Plant Breeding and Biotechnology INRA, Paris, France.

Ciceri, Piera, Milan University, Italy.

Clugston, Richard, CRLE and ULSF and the Earth Charter USA Campaign, Washington, DC, USA.

Corcoran, Peter Blaze, Florida Gulf Coast University, USA.

Corvers, Ron, Open University of the Netherlands, Heerlen, The Netherlands.

Fien, John, Griffith University, Brisbane, Australia.

Authors

Hubert, Bernard, Department of Agrarian Systems and Development, INRA, Paris, France.

Ivens, Wilfried P.M.F., Open University of the Netherlands, Heerlen, The Netherlands.

Jansen, J.L.A., Delft University of Technology, The Netherlands.

Johnston, Andy, Higher Education Partnership for Sustainability, London, UK.

Michelsen, Gerd, University of Lüneburg, Germany.

Roland, Marie-Claude, Young Researchers Training Programme, INRA, Paris, France.

Parkin, Sara, Forum for the Future, London, UK.

Seddon, Deborah, Forum for the Future, London, UK.

Setti, Fausta, Milan University, Italy.

van Dam-Mieras, Rietje, Open University of the Netherlands, Heerlen, and Scientific Council for Government Policy, The Hague, The Netherlands.

van Mansvelt, Emanuel Rogier, University of Amsterdam, The Netherlands.

Winkelmann, Hans-Peter, Secretary-General of COPERNICUS-CAMPUS, Dortmund, Germany.

Wissenschaft in gesellschaftlicher Verantwortung

Für ein vollständiges Verzeichnis der Titel dieser Reihe fordern Sie bitte den Sonderprospekt an.

REIHE
WISSENSCHAFT IN GESELLSCHAFTLICHER VERANTWORTUNG

Band 26:
Rolf Arnold: NATUR ALS VORBILD
– Selbstorganisation als Modell der Pädagogik,
ISBN 3-88864-126-8, 5 €

Band 34:
Klaus Sojka: UMWELTSCHUTZ UND UMWELTRECHT –
zur Unterrichtung und für die Praxis
ISBN 3-88864-134-9, 9 € (Doppelheft)

Band 36:
Dietmar Bolscho: UMWELTBEWUSSTSEIN ZWISCHEN ANSPRUCH UND WIRKLICHKEIT
– Anmerkungen zu einem Dilemma
ISBN 3-88864-136-5, 5 €

Band 39:
Ulrich Pfister, Guido Block-Künzler:
MITARBEITERBETEILIGUNG IM BETRIEBLICHEN UMWELTSCHUTZ – Erfahrungen – Vorschläge
ISBN 3-88864-140-3, 9 €

Band 44:
Horst Siebert: DER KONSTRUKTIVISMUS ALS PÄDAGOGISCHE WELTANSCHAUUNG – Entwurf einer konstruktivistischen Didaktik
ISBN 3-88864-144-6, 9 €

Band 42:
Günter Altner, Gerd Michelsen (Hg.):
ZUKÜNFTIGE ENERGIEPOLITIK
– Konsens jetzt!
ISBN 3-88864-142-X, 9 €

Verlag für Akademische Schriften
Wielandstraße 10 • 60316 Frankfurt
Telefon (069) 77 93 66 • Fax (069) 70 73 967
e-mail: info@vas-verlag.de • internet: www.vas-verlag.de

VAS

Reihe: Innovation in den Hochschulen – Nachhaltige Entwicklung

Herausgeber: Prof. Dr. Andreas Fischer, Prof. Dr. Gerd Michelsen und Prof. Dr. Ute Stoltenberg, Universität Lüneburg

Band 1:

Gerd Michelsen (Hrsg.)
Sustainable Universität
Auf dem Weg zu einem universitären Agendaprozeß
ISBN 3-88864-290-6 • 250 S. • 14 €

Band 2:
Ute Stoltenberg (Hrsg.)
Lebenswelt Hochschule
– Raum-Bildung, Konsum-Muster und Kommunikation für eine nachhaltige Entwicklung
ISBN 3-88864-310-4 • 181 S. • 14 €

Band 3:
Andreas Fischer (Hrsg.)
Vom schwierigen Vergnügen einer Kommunikation über die Idee der Nachhaltigkeit
ISBN 3-88864-311-2 • 235 S. • 14 €

Band 4:
Joachim Müller, Harald Gilch, Kai-Olaf Bastenhorst (Hrsg.)
Umweltmanagement an Hochschulen
Dokumentation eines Workshops von Januar 2001 an der Universität Lüneburg
ISBN 3-88864-315-5 • 187 S. • 14 €

Band 5:
Günter Altner, Gerd Michelsen (Hrsg.)
Ethik und Nachhaltigkeit
Grundsatzfragen und Handlungsperspektiven im universitäten Agendaprozess
ISBN 3-88864-321-X • Doppelband • 386 Seiten • 19,50 €

Band 6:
Andreas Fischer, Gabriela Hahn (Hrsg.)
Interdisziplinarität fängt im Kopf an
ISBN 3-88864-335-X • 187 S. • 14 €

Band 7:
Peter Paulus, Ute Stoltenberg
Agenda 21 und Universität
– auch eine Frage der Gesundheit
ISBN 3-88864-356-2 • 2002 • 170 Seiten • 14 €

Band 8:
Rietje van Dam-Mieras, Gerd Michelsen, Hans-Peter Winkelmann (Eds.)
COPERNICUS in Lüneburg
Higher Education in the Context of Sustainable Development and Globalization
ISBN 3-88864-357-0 • 252 Seiten • 2002 • 14 €

Sonderband:
Ute Stoltenberg/Eriuccio Nora (Ed.)
Lokale Agenda 21 / Agenda 21 Locale
– Akteure und Aktionen in Deutschland und Italien
– Attori ed Azioni in Germania ed in Italia
ISBN 3-88864-307-4 • 293 S. • 16,50 €

Weitere Informationen zur Reihe:
Innerhalb der kommenden zwei Jahre werden ca. acht bis zehn Bände erscheinen zu den Themenschwerpunkten: Umweltmanagementsystem • Energie • Lebenswelt Hochschule • Lehre & Interdisziplinarität • Nachhaltigkeit & Kunst • Information & Kommunikation • Internet

Abonnement:
Die Reihe kann auch beim Verlag abonniert werden – versandkostenfrei.

Verlag für Akademische Schriften
Wielandstraße 10 • 60316 Frankfurt
Telefon (069) 77 93 66 • Fax (069) 70 73 9 67
e-mail: info@vas-verlag.de • internet: www.vas-verlag.de

Ökologie • Gesundheitspolitik

ARBEITSGEMEINSCHAFT
ÖKOLOGISCHER LANDBAU (Hrsg.)
Leitfaden Ökologischer Landbau in Werkstätten für Behinderte
ISBN 3-88864-302-3 • Juni 2000 • Format DIN A 4 • 215 Seiten mit 110 Abbildungen und 8 Vierfarbtafeln • 22 €

Der Leitfaden liefert praxisnahe Hinweise, Beispielsbeschreibung und Checklisten, wie ein ökologisch bewirtschafteter Grüner Bereich im Rahmen einer Werkstatt für Behinderte optimiert oder neu eingerichtet werden kann, um zu einer Ausweitung der ökologisch bewirtschafteten Fläche im Rahmen von Werkstätten für Behinderte beizutragen.

Zum Herausgeber:
In dem 1988 gegründeten Dachverband sind Verbände des Ökologischen Landbaus organisiert, die unter Ökologischer Landwirtschaft mehr als nur den Verzicht auf Chemie verstehen: Demeter, Bioland, Biokreis, Naturland, ANOG, Eco Vin, Gäa, Ökosiegel, Biopark. Sie berücksichtigen den Zusammenhang zwischen landwirtschaftlicher Erzeugung, gesunder Ernährung und Erhalt der Kulturlandschaft. Sie setzen Ökologischen Landbau konsequent um, indem sämtliche Betriebsflächen und -zweige in die ökologische Bewirtschaftung eines Hofs einbezogen werden.

Alf Trojan, Heiner Legewie
Nachhaltige Gesundheit und Entwicklung
Leitbilder, Politik und Praxis der Gestaltung gesundheitsförderlicher Umwelt- und Lebensbedingungen
ISBN 3-88864-299-X • 2001 • 436 S.
• 27,50 €

Welche Visionen und Leitbilder können zu Beginn des 21. Jahrhunderts das Leben der Bürger und die Ziele der gesellschaftlichen Kräfte bestimmen? Anders gefragt: Wie wollen wir und unsere Kinder im neuen Jahrhundert leben? Welche Weichen wollen wir für die Lebensbedingungen unserer Kinder stellen?
Von der breiten Öffentlichkeit weitgehend unbeachtet, wurden in den letzten 20 Jahren von den Vereinten Nationen (UN) zwei eng miteinander zusammenhängende konkrete Utopien entwickelt und in ermutigenden Beispielen erprobt, die weder der Vorwurf ideologischer Einengung noch mangelnder Umsetzbarkeit trifft: das Leitbild der Weltgesundheitsorganisation (WHO) „Nachhaltige Gesundheit für alle" sowie das Leitbild der Konferenz von Rio „Nachhaltige Entwicklung" (sustainable development).
Durch die Projekte „Gesunde Städte" und „Lokale Agenda 21" werden diese Leitbilder und weitere Ansätze zur Stärkung gesundheitsförderlicher Lebensbedingungen seit mehr als einem Jahrzehnt in aller Welt erfolgreich erprobt, sodass inzwischen ein gesicherter Wissensfundus zur Umsetzung vorliegt. Das Buch liefert erstmals eine Gesamtdarstellung dieser Entwicklung und der Erfahrungen bei der Umsetzung der Leitbilder.

Verlag für Akademische Schriften
Wielandstraße 10 • 60316 Frankfurt
Telefon (069) 77 93 66 • Fax (069) 707 39 67
e-mail: info@vas-verlag.de • internet: www.vas-verlag.de